On a Wing and a Prayer
with Good Morning Sunday

On a Wing and a Prayer

with Good Morning Sunday

Compiled by
Rosemary Foxcroft

With a Foreword by Don Maclean

CANTERBURY
PRESS
Norwich

© BBC 2004

First published in 2004 by the Canterbury Press Norwich
(a publishing imprint of Hymns Ancient & Modern
Limited, a registered charity)
St Mary's Works, St Mary's Plain,
Norwich, Norfolk, NR3 3BH

www.scm-canterburypress.co.uk

British Library Cataloguing in Publication data

A catalogue record for this book is available
from the British Library

ISBN 1-85311-481-2

Typeset in Scala by Regent Typesetting, London
Printed and bound by
Biddles Ltd, www.biddles.co.uk

Contents

Foreword

To infinity and beyond

Reading this book has forced me to remember the many people we've interviewed over the past fourteen years on Good Morning Sunday. Of course, they are not all in the book, but let me tell you about them. They've been a varied lot and I must say I've been genuinely interested in all of them. I've been overcome with hero worship when speaking to great sportsmen like Gareth Edwards, Gavin Hastings, Jahangir Khan and Jonathan Edwards. I was like a lovelorn schoolboy when I interviewed Reba McEntire and Dolly Parton. I'm desperately in love with them both! Please don't ask me to choose between them, though the fact that Reba sent me a thank you card after I interviewed her the first time might just swing it. I'm a fan of country and western music and have met so many country superstars like Kenny Rogers, Crystal Gayle, Mary Chapin Carpenter and Tricia Yearwood – what a job I've got!

Of course we've interviewed a few people I've not liked very much. I could name six total megalomaniacs but I won't. There are those determined to put over their agenda. Ludovic Kennedy has total belief in non-belief. Everytime I mentioned God he interrupted me saying, 'God? What do you mean? I don't understand what you mean by the word God.' In the end I was fed up and said, 'If you don't understand the word God why did you call your book *Farewell to God*?'

Some interviewees have been overcome with emotion. Sam Salt, Captain of HMS Sheffield, fought back tears as he spoke of the loss of his ship in Falkland waters fifteen years earlier. Arthur Titherington who, as a prisoner of the Japanese, spent four years down a mine in the Far East, relived the horror as he related it to me. The father of Lieutenant David Tinker RN, who published his son's letters in a book which became the best-selling piece of Falklands War literature, found it impossible to talk about his son without weeping and I realised that life had ended for him too when his boy was lost in May 1982. Most recently I saw tears in the eyes of Chelsea Pensioner, Vic Massingham, as he recalled his part in the Battle of Arnhem exactly 60 years ago.

We've been to some great houses, Mrs Foxtrot and I. We visited Glen Campbell in Phoenix where his house has a magnificent fountain in the shape of his guitar. We went down to Rye to interview Spike Milligan. As we drew up outside we both said, 'What a dreadful-looking house.' We got to the front door and immediately beneath the bellpush was a plaque which read, 'This house designed by the blind architect.' Ranulph Fiennes invited us to his home. Despite the freezing weather, all windows were open wide and the great explorer stood there in a short-sleeved, open-neck shirt. We also went to interview The Princess Royal at Buckingham Palace; that's quite a nice house too.

Many interviewees come up with little gems as this book illustrates. When I asked Kate Adie what went through her mind when she was pinned down in a war zone unable to move, she replied, 'I think, if this goes on much longer, have I packed enough knickers?' Roy Castle was undergoing chemotherapy the last time I interviewed him. 'Are you upset that you've lost all your hair?' I asked. 'Not at all, it means I can go to fancy dress parties as a roll-on deodorant.' I still miss him now. When I asked Sir Bernard Lovell if science disproved the existence of God, he replied, 'On the contrary, the more I delve into the universe the more I'm convinced that God must exist.'

John Denver longed to travel in space he told me. He was eager to talk to me about flying. 'So you've got a Tomahawk,' he said, 'great plane.' 'What have you got?' I asked. 'A Pitts Special [fully aerobatic bi-plane] and a Lear Jet,' he replied. Sadly he died at the controls of an experimental light aircraft but somehow I think that's the way he would have wanted to go.

There have been other wonderful American guests like Larry Hagman who insisted on providing ten-gallon hats for both he and I when Rosemary brought out the camera. Garth Brooks' manager had told me not to mention God or religion during the interview with him. 'It's an aspect of Garth that needs to be purged from his image.' 'Garth, do you believe that your voice is a gift from God?' was my very first question. The manager was furious but Garth afterwards thanked me for giving him the opportunity to share his faith. Then there were the Osmonds, both Merrill and Jimmy, who greeted me like a long-lost friend though I'd never met them. They were one of the first pop acts to produce videos to promote their record releases. We used to show these as part of Crackerjack. The entire show would then be recorded by the record company in England and sent back to USA for viewing by the brothers who consequently felt that they knew me.

Archbishop Desmond Tutu was probably my happiest interviewee. If you chance to meet him don't play any music or he'll start dancing. Yasser Arafat was very happy too until I asked him a dodgy question and then he changed dramatically.

I'm probably best at interviewing what Rosemary refers to as 'women of a certain age'. My conquests, according to her, include authors Barbara Taylor Bradford, Jackie Collins, Joanna Trollope, Susan Howatch and P. D. James who squeezed my hand and said, 'Oh Don, call me Phyllis'. There were ladies from the world of showbusiness who also melted to my charm if Rosemary is to be believed: Nana Mouskouri, Eartha Kitt, Janet Suzman, Liv Ullmann, Judith Durham, who wrote afterwards to say it was the best interview she'd ever done and the lovely Linda Gray of Dallas fame who was about to appear naked on stage in The Graduate, but refrained from giving me a personal preview.

I've experienced danger as when I interviewed Topol while he was having dinner. I sat opposite him and he talked constantly while he ate. I spent the next hour picking sweet corn off my shirt-front. I've also courted danger. My interview with Bill Wyman provoked several letters saying 'How dare you have a serial philanderer on a religious programme?', Jim Davidson was another risky choice, his reputation as a blue comic went before him but Jim is an erudite man and a man seeking a spiritual path. I received dozens of letters saying 'I've never liked Jim Davidson before, but now I see him in a completely different light.' Jim spoke of being involved in freemasonry which upset many listeners though not nearly so many as Hugh Pinnock who had come over from Salt Lake City to take charge of the Mormon Church in Great Britain. He was a delightful man who had a voice like my boyhood cowboy hero, Hopalong Cassidy, but my listeners branded him a cult leader and chastised us for inviting him on.

We've interviewed foreign royalty – Queen Noor of Jordan, a truly classic beauty, and also Prince Hassan. There were several disappointed listeners that week (they thought I'd said

'Princess Anne'), and we've spoken to presidents: Vaclav Havel of the Czech Republic and Glafcos Clerides of Cyprus.

I've been humbled to meet such people as John McCarthy for whom we all prayed while he was held hostage, James Mawdesley who took on the Government of Burma single-handedly, Lisa Potts who protected the toddlers in her charge from a machete-wielding madman. I was equally humbled to be in the same room as Leonard Cheshire VC, the holiest layman I've ever encountered, and to get the very last interview with Professor Christiaan Barnard, the one man I've met whom I can guarantee will still be an encyclopaedia entry a thousand years from now.

But the two interviewees who've impressed me most are both women. Heather Reynolds who is caring for over eight hundred Aids orphans in Southern Africa and Joni Eareckson Tada, paralysed from the shoulders down, spending every day in an electric wheelchair yet having the most perfect faith and submitting totally to the will of God. 'Be it done unto me according to Thy word.' If only we were all able and willing to say that.

Rosemary has spent long hours recalling words spoken or sometimes spilt on a Sunday morning with which to fill these pages. They come from men and women of many nationalities and many faiths, some feted as celebrities, some very ordinary but all VIPs as far as we're concerned. I hope they amuse, inspire or just make you think and rest assured that we shall continue to try to find really interesting interview subjects for Good Morning Sunday.

Don Maclean
September 2004

Part 1

The Spiritual Journey

Being a Christian

My faith is important to me. How could it not be? What I'm always anxious to avoid is sounding sanctimonious or priggish, or sounding as though I think that, because I am a Catholic or a Christian, that somehow invests my political ideas with some superior quality that other people don't have. When people who are practising Christians sound like that when they are talking politics, I sometimes think that puts people off becoming members of Christian Churches.

But having said that, it is the most important part of my life; it has been a very important part of the socio-cultural part of my life. If I was going to write about my childhood a lot of it would be about going to church as a little altar boy when I was seven or eight. I can still pretty well say the mass in Latin from all those responses when I was a kid with Father Canning up on the altar, or Father O'Sullivan. This was pre-Vatican II. I remember the hell-fire sermons that used to be preached when we had the parish retreat every year, being taken along to service for a mass and a redemptionist sermon. That part of religion has played an important part in my memories. And I think, as you get older, you do start to realize that religion helps to avoid life and the prospect of death being bleak. I would find it very difficult not to be a Christian – not to believe. It

[3]

would leave a terrible void in my life and I think it would make me very worried about the future.

Chris Patten, politician

Ingredients for life

You really need three things in life: someone to love, something to do and something to look forward to.

Kenny Rogers, singer and songwriter

A way of life

Being a Hindu is more of a way of life than anything else. I was raised a Hindu by my mum and my dad. I read all the mythology and said all the prayers, but now it's more about being a good person: it's not about being forced to go to the temple every week.

Anoushka Shankar, musician

What is important

I learnt so much. You don't realize how much prejudice you do have in your life, growing up in a certain religious field I suppose. We didn't get married for three and a half years and it was very important because we really needed to go down a road to understand what we wanted and to find out what was important in our religion. It really is a shame how much we have taken God's word and put it into so many categories, and I look at the simplistic way of how Jesus loves us and how he wants us to be. It can be part of everything in your life by remembering he's there with you all the time. It's not about going to mass on a Sunday and forgetting him for the rest of the week.

Máire Brennan, singer and songwriter

God in all things

Teach me, my God and King,
　　in all things thee to see;
and what I do in anything
　　to do it as for thee.

George Herbert (1593–1633)

Mistakes

You don't have to make the same mistakes as other people. Watch what they do and try not to do it.

Alvin Hall, financial guru

Defined by my culture

Every day I would go to normal secular school from eight in the morning to three o'clock in the afternoon. Then I'd get on the bus and go to Hebrew school from four to six. And then I was in temple on Saturdays, and then I went to Hebrew-speaking camp and then I was Bar'Mitzvahed. By the time I was fourteen I didn't want to be Jewish any more. I'd had it. I'd had enough of it, and I went about my life just being a normal teenager. Then I met my wife and we fell in love. And all of a sudden, I wanted to have a religious ceremony when we got married because my feelings for my wife were so deep and so great that I wanted to do something which was past what I understood. And past what I understand is something which is called religious, whatever that means. Then I had my children. And so much of who I am is defined by my culture – the holidays, the family celebrations, the food, the meals; it defined who I am today.

And I wanted to give that definition also to my children.

Mandy Patinkin, singer

[Jesus said,] 'Truly I tell you, whoever does not receive the kingdom of God as a little child will never enter it.'

Mark 10.15

Multi-faith society

My father comes from a Jewish family; it wasn't a religious Jewish family – they were very secular, non-religious people. My father was born in Germany but they moved to Czechoslovakia in his late twenties when my grandfather took up a place as Professor of Ancient History at Prague University. My father's family were fortunate, they managed to get out in 1939 and came to Britain. And my father married my mother, who is not Jewish.

My upbringing wasn't religious in any sense but my parents

were careful to introduce me to the idea of faith. I went to a C of E primary school. I'm very happy to have learnt quite a bit about the Christian tradition because it forms perhaps the largest foundation of what is now our multi-faith and multi-cultured society. I still like to hear hymns although I wouldn't force them on kids now, but I am glad we had to sing them in a way.

Ben Elton, comedian and writer

To have life

It is fantastic to have life; to have five senses; to wake up in the morning and have a free day. It is fantastic and it is way above average.

Art Garfunkel, singer and songwriter

All we have is this moment

I do meditation every day. It really does keep us in the present moment. Because so many of us, and I am including myself in that, think of what happened yesterday. We think of the 'to do' lists. We think of tomorrow and the future and what if this and what if that. All we have is this moment. This moment I'm here speaking to you. That's all we have and meditation for me is the quieting of all the chatter; it's a quieting of the mind. It's being in touch with who you are: your core essence. Who are you? What is my connection with the universe? Is this some big jig-saw puzzle? Do we all have some means of participating? What is our participation? Do we have one heartbeat?

One heartbeat

When September 11th happened, I felt innately that we were all New Yorkers. There was one heartbeat. And I think when you experience that, you experience your own essence. That's the reason why I meditate.

Linda Gray, actor

Then I know he exists

When I'm working, I feel close to God. Then I know he exists. When I'm not working, it's a question of belief. I remember being in Greece over one winter and the music seemed to be coming from nowhere. Obviously I've been trained as a musician, I've been trained as a composer in the Western style, but the music seemed to be just coming out of me. And it did appear that it was being divinely dictated. I don't know where it was coming from.

John Tavener, composer

Only one mouth

My grandmother used to say, 'Son, you've got two eyes, two ears and one mouth, for a very good reason. Say nothin' until you hear more.'

Bill Cullen

Great works

Much silence and a good disposition, there are no two works better than those.

From the Hadith

Music and icons

According to Orthodox traditions, icon painting stems from St Luke's painting of the Mother of God, so all paintings of her, in some way, are a variant of that original. And the same applies to the icon of Christ. I think it was the King of Odessa who asked if Christ would come and see him, and Christ made the imprint of his face on a cloth and it was sent to him. And he was cured. Then from that time and from the shroud, which was originally in Constantinople and is now in Turin, we take the prototype of Christ. You're supposed to fast while you're painting an icon, you're supposed to go to communion as frequently as possible and I do regard writing music as a bit like icon painting.

John Tavener, composer

Shared teachings

The teachings of Jesus are very similar to the teachings I follow. They're called Vaishnav, within Hinduism. It's a monotheistic belief in a personal God, and Christ seemed to be teaching that: love the Lord thy Father with all your heart. I find that inspiring and it seems to me teachings of all the great saints,

[9]

great prophets, be it Moses, be it Christ, be it Muhammad, be it the Asidav, who happens to be the Hindu authority, are very similar. They may be interpreted differently.

Krishna Dharma, Hindu priest and writer

The test of experience

(*It seems that where Buddhism parts company with the teachings of Jesus, is that Jesus was very much rooted in this world, whereas in a sense the Buddha taught detachment from the world.*)

Buddhism uses the metaphor of the lotus growing from mud. You've got this image of a spiritual experience – something that has a beauty and a purity, but the fact of the matter is for the lotus to grow, its roots are in the mud. I think Buddhism doesn't have a transcendent spirituality. There's a verse in one of the Zen texts which says: this very place the lotus paradise, this very body the Buddha. The idea is that the real meaning of spiritual practice is something that you must discover within experience.

For me the teaching of Jesus is something that gets its authority not because it's scriptural but to the extent that you can interact with it, to the extent that you can engage with it and test it with your own experience.

Dhammarati, senior member of the Western Buddhist Order

Influences on the mind

We tend to think we are born with all we've got and we can't change it: that the genes are all important. The truth is that nurture and our environment are incredibly important with this most important of all organs, the mind.

Robert Winston, scientist

The heart

(*Reading from the letters of a Sufi master.*)

When the heart is moved the limbs move also and when it is still they are likewise still;
> If it arises, they arise; if it sits, they sit, if it becomes contracted, so do they contract;
> If it relaxes they also relax; if it weakens, they weaken and if it is strong they are strong; if it is humble they become humble;
> If it is proud, they become proud and so forth.

Read by Abdullah Trevathan, Headteacher of Islamia School

[Jesus] called the crowd with his disciples, and said to them, 'If any want to become my followers, let them deny themselves and take up their cross and follow me. For those who want to save their life will lose it, and those who lose their life for my sake, and for the sake of the gospel, will save it. For what will it profit them to gain the whole world and forfeit their life?'

Mark 8.34–6

The Annunciation

On the feast of the Annunciation, we commemorate the day on which the Angel Gabriel told the Blessed Virgin Mary that she was to become the mother of Christ. We pray that we, too, may submit to your will in all things, Lord, and be ever willing to say, 'Be it done unto me according to thy word.'

Don Maclean

Infallible wisdom

When you're eighteen or nineteen, it's the only time in your life you know everything.

Melvyn Bragg, writer and broadcaster

God-given emotions

I have been looking at the whole concept of worship, the response that happens on the inside and how it reflects on the outside. The one thing that always defeats me is that, on a Saturday afternoon, on any given football ground in England, you see people jump and shout and cry and laugh for a game of football, and you put those same people in a church setting and you see this whole thing, 'I am not allowed to respond with the joy that I had.' I believe God gave us these emotions, and there are only several ways as humans we can respond; and I believe that all the responses that we have that God has given us naturally to cry, to laugh, to jump and to feel the joy and elation and to feel the sorrow and sadness, they are all legitimate ways of bringing worship to God.

Noel Robinson, worship leader

Contributing with a sense of self

Children who have a strong sense of self – a positive sense of who they are and what their culture is – make for positive and participating citizens. That's what we see now almost after twenty years of having this school. People who have a strong sense of who they are are also people who want to contribute. It's those who don't have a sense of self and have an identity crisis who may revert to a form of fundamentalism.

Abdullah Trevathan, Headteacher of Islamia School

No reason to quit

Success is no reason to quit.

Kenny Rogers, singer and songwriter

'Is now, always was and always will be'

(*Talking about his experience during his recent operation.*)

All the prayers in most religions that I've researched have a term 'is now, always was and always will be'. And that to me is what you really are. You are always, you always have been and you always will be. This stage of your life is one of the levels of existence and there are many levels. And the next level, I found, during my operation, the next level is love: pure unadulterated love. It's the most wonderful feeling, and very familiar. All these things are very familiar when you enter them. You think it's going to be foreign country, but it ain't. You've been there before. You're going to be there always. It's a wonderful experience.

Larry Hagman, actor

Let there be no compulsion in religion: Truth stands out clear from Error: whoever rejects Evil and believes in Allah hath grasped the most trustworthy hand-hold, that never breaks. And Allah heareth and knoweth all things.

Qur'an 2.256

A metaphor that moves

(*Christians believe that Jesus rose again from the dead. What does a Buddhist believe?*)

There's a story about an enlightened Zen teacher and he was asked what happened to him after death. His disciples are all sitting round expecting to hear from somebody enlightened and he said: 'I don't know.' And they were mystified and said, 'What do you mean you don't know, you're an enlightened Zen master'; and he said, 'Yes, but I'm not a dead enlightened Zen master.'

I have no idea whether Jesus rose from the dead. I have to say I don't think it's likely. I guess I would go to the allegory, trying to point to something of transcendent importance, trying to suggest there's a level of experience, a level of reality that's bigger and deeper. You can't but be moved by the metaphor.

Dhammarati, senior member of the Western Buddhist Order

Divine intervention

I'm not an overtly religious person but I believe sometimes in divine intervention. When you're a musician, an artist or a writer, you might ask where it's all coming from. I prefer to use the word God. Everyone has the sense, a feeling that there's a higher power, and I just tapped into it. That's where I get my inspiration from.

Lionel Richie, singer and songwriter

Be still

Be still for the Spirit of the Lord, the Holy One, is here.
Come, bow before him now, with reverence and fear.
In him no sin is found, we stand on holy ground.
Be still, for the Spirit of the Lord, the Holy One, is here.

David J. Evans (b. 1957)

The solitary way

(*About the Celtic saints.*)

I was a very strong Christian, I came from the North of England, I knew about Lindsifarne, I'd been to Iona, I knew the Roman Wall region, and a lot of these saints had travelled in that territory; they had lived there so I felt they were part of my own past. Also they were interested in scholarship, which I was. So those three things – the fact it was to do with Christianity, it was to do with the North of England and North of Scotland, and it was to do with learning – attracted me to them. And the more I was attracted, I got to them, the more fantastic they are of course, as individuals, men and women, because there were a lot of women saints in the so-called Dark Ages.

I think that in that time they saw themselves in the North of Ireland, in the North of England and Scotland as being the second lot of the apostles; there had been the apostles, then seven centuries later there were these people, who actually tried to be like the apostles. And in the eyes of those who followed, they very nearly succeeded. They made prophecies like the apostles did, they caused miracles to happen, they spoke in different languages, they converted pagan tribes to Christianity, they were martyred for their faith, which happened to some of the apostles. So they followed in a path of the apostles and they were extremely powerful and influential and I like the fact that they came out of a Celtic past, which meant that, although they were indeed Christians and followers of Christ, they still retained a great deal of Celtic thought and they understood that spirits could be in the water, the air and the sea and so on. They believed in the individual and not the organization.

The Celts liked to roam free, where the Roman Church said no, it has to be organized, there have to be hierarchies, there have to be bishops and there have to be great abbeys and so forth, we must do it this way. And the Celts stood out for that isolated, individual, often solitary way, which I find very attractive.

Melvyn Bragg, writer and broadcaster

He who protects virtue is himself protected by it, but he who destroys virtue is himself utterly destroyed.

Mahabharata

Last Sunday of Advent

We rejoice at the thought of the birth of your son, Jesus Christ. Grant that, as we receive him as our redeemer, we may joyfully behold him when he shall come to be our judge.

Don Maclean

When I was at school

I was very, very religious when I was at school and I really enjoyed the assembly in the morning, singing hymns. This was just hymn-singing, but I found it very peaceful. I'm basically what you call in England, 'C of E', but at one time I went to a Methodist church that was run by David Frost's father. I remember David in his purple school uniform. I used to love going there and I used to force my mother to go. As I went into art college I gradually stopped going, but I always go to midnight mass at Westminster Abbey and I don't feel Christmas is Christmas without doing that.

Zandra Rhodes, fashion designer

God, the only reality

(*Reading from the letters of a Sufi master.*)

Those who've made their way to God, who have died to themselves in contemplation of God's infinity and freed themselves from the illusion that there is any reality other than God. Such people find that existence follows them and obeys them; wherever they turn it turns and God is our warning for what we say.

Read by Abdullah Trevathan, Headteacher of Islamia School

Not unquestioning

I rejected Christianity and parenthood and everything I could think of. In the sixties and the seventies it was a struggle to maintain any connection whatsoever. And I'm certainly not the besotted unquestioning Christian I was in the forties and fifties.

(*Do you regret that?*)

Yes, but then I regret that I'm no longer an 11-year-old bowling along the streets with a hoop. There you are.

Melvyn Bragg, writer and broadcaster

The pillars of your life

The tenets of the faith stay with you no matter what. They are the pillars of your life.

Beverley Knight, soul singer

Made for . . .

We have been made for goodness, we have been made for transcendence, we have been made for God.

Desmond Tutu, former Archbishop of Cape Town

In the presence of God

(*Phone call to Cardinal Basil Hume on Sunday 31 August 1997, the morning Princess Diana died.*)

Shock, after a little time, gives way to a deep sadness. When we are in shock we just have to be in the presence of God, recognizing, yes, yes, he is present. Whenever we experience death, especially in a family, then we ask ourselves very fundamental questions: is it the end? where is she now? The horror of it. We

[19]

find our consolations by saying, 'Yes, we can't accept that life in this world is all that we have. There is something beyond.' And death we see as a gateway: a gateway to something which is lovely and best for all of us. But at the present time we just have to be, as it were, in the presence of God. And it is not a bad prayer just to pop into a church, just to sit or to kneel and just absorb the reality, and absorb it in the presence of God.

Basil Hume, former Cardinal Archbishop of Westminster

Prayer is ...

Prayer is the soul's sincere desire,
    uttered or unexpressed;
the motion of a hidden fire
    that trembles in the breast.

James Montgomery (1771–1854)

I say a prayer

I say a prayer, just to say thanks, keep me safe, get me through this, not even ask to win, just help me achieve and do the best I can do. If the best means I win, that's great. If the best means I come eighth, that's great too.

Darren Campbell, athlete, 200m silver medallist

Fully alive

Praying is about being fully alive.

Ruth Scott, Anglican priest

Seeing through faith

We always felt it was a matter of simply having faith or not having faith; if you could accept the inexplicable things of life and believe there was some sort of pattern and reason for them then we would think it would be easier to accept Jesus Christ. But we think when you see the things of life and you can't see any pattern and you can't see any reason then your faith is lacking.

The Proclaimers, Scottish singers and songwriters

Power in praise

I keep on praising God. I remember even the day I found out I was HIV-positive, there was this peace within me that came and said, 'Yes, thank you Lord'. You know I keep on saying it wherever I go because I realize there is power in praise. Because I think if you question God, you'll be waiting for an answer, you'll be dragging yourself with so many things that it may even get your energy. I realize that the more I worship him, the more I thank him. I realize that he does more good things in my life. I think people need to understand that there is power when you can praise.

Princess Zulu, Zambian AIDS orphan and
now international spokesperson on AIDS

You're accepted as you are

I have spent a lot of time in the past few years just finding old churches of whatever denomination, just going into them and wondering about things. I get a lot of comfort from reading the Bible. My grandmother and my mother go to chapel regularly and I was brought up as a Welsh Baptist. That whole rich background of hymn-singing – I'd never want to do without that. 'Arglwydd Dyma Fi' (Here I am, Lord) is my old time favourite melody and the lyric on top just makes it astoundingly powerful. My grandmother and mother used to sing it. It's a hymn that just forgives all your human weaknesses and all your sinful behaviour and it says you're accepted as you are, completely, and I think that is so powerful.

Cerys Matthews, singer and songwriter

My faith has always been very important

Before every game I pray. I pray to God to give me strength and make me give 100 per cent. After the World Cup, the whole team went to Mecca. It was very spiritual. The minute we arrived, we literally were about to cry. It was the best feeling I have ever had.

The school I went to was a Christian school. We used to go once a week to sing hymns in church.

Wasim Akram, former Pakistan and Lancashire cricketer

Lunch at No. 10

John Major (then Prime Minister) put on a little lunch at No. 10 for the President of Israel and when it came to the lunch we remembered that we hadn't told them about one thing: in Judaism if you're going to make a blessing over food, the food has got to be there. And no one had explained that. So at the lunch, John Major stood up and said, 'I now call on the Chief Rabbi to say grace', and everyone stood up and there was half the British Cabinet and the President of Israel looking at me and there was nothing to say grace over. This was a major diplomatic incident in the making. So I lifted my eyes up to the hills looking for salvation, and out of the corner of my eye I could see someone had draped a bunch of grapes around a table ornament. It was the only bit of food in the whole room, so I made a blessing upon a grape, and honour was saved. Afterwards I said to the Prime minister, you've got to understand your faith is different from ours. You have more faith than we do. You are prepared to thank God for that which we are about to receive. We, after long experience, prefer to have received it first.

Jonathan Sacks, the Chief Rabbi

Defining myself as a human being

As time has gone on, I've focused less and less about defining myself as being Asian and more about defining myself as a human being. And I think the time for marginalizing people on the basis of racial heritage is over.

Nitin Sawhney, writer and musician

The key to everything

The more I think about it the more I think forgiveness is the key to everything. But until we're ready to claim the fact that we are perpetrators as well as victims, I mean it's much more comfortable to be a victim.

Kathleen Griffin, writer

The need to question

If you don't question what was written long ago you'll just be in one mess after another. It doesn't fit at all into the world, as we now know it. It doesn't measure up to the responsibilities we now have. We are actually turning out, God help us, to be very rarely in the image of God.

David Jenkins, former Bishop of Durham

A certain energy

(*So you're a firm believer in life after death?*)

Not life as we know it. Not in this physical form. It's like that you're never dead. You are never dead because you never have been. Have you ever seen the aurora borealis? I equate it to that curtain of energy, you see, a changing light. I guess you see it here in England a lot. And that's how I envisage all of us. A kind of electronic curtain that is flowing all the time for ever: energy.

Larry Hagman, actor

Lord, cleanse my sins

The noblest wonders here we view,
     in souls renewed and sins forgiven:
Lord, cleanse my sins, my soul renew,
     and make thy word my guide to heaven.

Isaac Watts (1674–1748)

Allah loveth not that evil should be noised abroad in public speech, except where injustice hath been done; for Allah is He Who haveth and knoweth all things.

Whether ye publish a good deed or conceal it or cover evil with pardon, verily, Allah doth blot out (sins) and hath power (in the judgement of values).

Qur'an 4.148–9

The power of passion

Many people don't know the positive power of passion, instead they are afraid of it. I believe passion is God inspired.

Rhonda Britton, self-help guru

The first step of forgiveness

Justice is crucial. I do workshops on forgiveness and the first thing that people ask is, 'If I forgive this person they would have got away with it.' Because I think we all need to feel we have our day in court in our heads. And we all have this fantasy that someone is going to come along and say, 'I was wrong, yes, I'm sorry.' And I think the first step of forgiveness is to let go of that hope: that forgiveness is never about the other person. It's always about yourself and you are the only person who can change in forgiveness.

Kathleen Griffin, writer

Moral character

The traits of the Sufi's moral character are long-suffering, humility, brotherly admonition, tender-hearted sympathy, magnanimity, fraternal concordance, beneficence, kindly moderation, self-sacrifice, service, warmth of heart, cheerful joviality, generosity, chivalry, relinquishing one's place for the sake of others, manliness, harmlessness, charity, forgiveness, faithfulness, modesty, gentleness, freshness of countenance and openness of face, pleasantry in speech, calm even-temperedness, remembering others in prayers of benediction, good humour, dispassionateness, reverence for brethren, veneration of masters, benevolence towards inferiors and superiors alike, treating as a trifle whatever pertains to themselves while magnifying and revering the obligations that others impose on them.

From *Adab al-Muridin – The Conduct of Seekers*,
a manual of Sufi discipline

Dare to stand alone

My father used to say to me: dare to be a Daniel, dare to stand alone. Dare to have a purpose.

Tony Benn, politician

Living in the last days

I'm on my knees all the time. Just for my own soul and for the souls of my children, my friends and my family because I truly believe we are living in the last days. If I'm right then everything that I do needs to be done around that God-centred philosophy because otherwise why would I want to be out here risking my life to the temptations of the world and the risks that go along with it; I'd be home in Utah fishing.

Merrill Osmond, singer and songwriter

Delivered from fear of death

The Christian faith and our Lord deliver you from fear of death. You see that death is a door opening into, rather than an ogre to be feared. To have that radically dealt with is one of the great results of the Christian faith. One is realistic enough to know that one's faculties get less and the way through may be difficult, but the fear of death itself, no, I think that is conquered.

Donald Coggan, former Archbishop of Canterbury

Hiding in a cavern

(*On those who don't question the Bible.*)

They want to hide, you see, from the world which has developed with science, worldwide globalization and all sorts of other faiths now equally around, in a sort of constructed cavern which they have made out of biblical texts.

David Jenkins, former Bishop of Durham

Working out your faith

I was aware that being a platform Christian and a sportsman people lionize and put you up there and expect you to tell your Christian story over and over again. It's a very dangerous place, because if you are a Christian you have got to go on growing, you can't stop and just get stuck. Part of what living and working in East London did for me was to say that you've got to stop being a platform Christian, you've got to be a Christian in this neighbourhood and work out your faith here.

David Sheppard, former Bishop of Liverpool

Facing difficulties

I have a philosophy that one should be able to stand up and face difficulties without the slightest provocation of invoking the help of the good Lord. I have been brought up to believe that you can meet most of your difficulties. But I must tell you something, when I jumped out over Hamburg, at night and with the flak coming up, I did two things. One, I said a prayer as I was going down. And the second thing, I was holding my pockets because inside my pockets were all my escaping kits and I didn't want to lose them. But the prayer came first. So, despite my upbringing that you must face your difficulties, there is a time when you have to invoke the help of the good Lord.

President Clerides of Cyprus

Surely this commandment that I am commanding you today is not too hard for you, nor is it too far away. It is not in heaven, that you should say, 'Who will go up to heaven for us, and get it for us so that we may hear and observe it?' Neither is it beyond the sea, that you should say, 'Who will cross to the other side of the sea for us, and get it for us so that we may hear it and observe it?' No, the word is very near to you; it is in your mouth and in your heart for you to observe.

Deuteronomy 30.11–14

I firmly believe

I am a great believer. I think probably that's why I'm a happy man. Because I do believe, firmly believe. I know about the spirit world. I know it exists and I know that God exists and Jesus Christ exists and that's a marvellous secure feeling to have.

John Mills, actor

Sacred art

I think the icon is the most sacred, the most transcendent art that exists and that's why I say that art critics have enormous difficulty with icons. Lord Clark, in his book on civilization, doesn't even mention icons. It's almost as if they can't cope with the icon, because you either have to fall down before it, or you're deeply moved by it, or it means absolutely nothing to you whatsoever.

John Tavener, composer

In love with mystery

I think we're supposed to be doubtful, to be constantly in a state of wonder at the mystery of it all, and in love with the mystery of it all.

Art Garfunkel, singer and songwriter

Art and revelation

(*Can anyone get as much out of say a beautiful Italian religious painting that they can get from an icon?*)

I certainly can from the very early, say the twelfth or thirteenth century, Italian. I lose them completely once they go into Renaissance because the artist's ego begins to take over. You see how clever he is, rather than how beautiful is Christ; how beautiful is the Mother of God. You cease to think that from then onwards, all the way up to Francis Bacon and to *An*

Unmade Bed. Some modern critics actually called this the new metaphysics. Well if this is the new metaphysics, all I can say is that I preferred the old one.

John Tavener, composer

Social teaching of Jesus

Well, I go to church but my own conviction is that what used to be called justification by works is what you do and not what you believe in. Justification by faith. And for me the mysteries of religion aren't helpful. I have respect for those who believe in them, but the social message of Jesus, the social teaching of Jesus, is tremendously important.

Tony Benn, politician

Stand back from the fray

The best politicians are those who are able to stand back from the fray. You don't have to go back too far to remember the days of Harold Macmillan who used to read novels in the garden of No. 10. And Churchill, while he was an active politician, used to write great histories. It wasn't that they were not doing their job properly. Actually, what it did was make them able to get a perspective on what they do.

Michael Dobbs, writer

True appreciation

Did you catch the programme on Michael Jackson? What a lot of money that man has, and what a lot he could do with it. Thoughts of money and wealth always remind me of when I first came across Buddhism in Glasgow. In a relaxed moment in between meditations over a cup of tea, a Buddhist teacher was chatting to me, and passed a comment about this sports car he really liked. I was a bit disturbed at this outward gushing of worldly materialism. I had assumed that these Buddhists only had their minds on higher things and had embraced poverty as the true way to enlightenment.

The teacher explained that he didn't expect to ever own the car, but it didn't stop him appreciating it. That answer eased my mind for a moment until he went on to say that he saw no nobility in poverty. In fact he went on to say you need money to put food in your belly, clothes on your back, and a roof over your head.

Dharmacari Nagaraja,
member of the Western Buddhist Order

Have a great life

You can have a great life on any income: what you need is imagination and resourcefulness, and a little discipline.

Alvin Hall, financial guru

The stuff of human life

We each strive to find peace and happiness, as individuals and as countries, trying to find meaning in uncertainty. How we do this is the stuff of human life. Ever since the dawn of time man has struggled with two great principles. In every moment we find we have a choice to act either by negating life with violence, greed and hatred, or by affirming life through love, generosity and compassion. From the Buddhist point of view, living your life merely from selfish self-interest makes us less than human, but if you choose to act with love, compassion and non-violence, this takes you closer to being truly human. This is the choice that every one can make at every moment of their life, regardless of one's particular circumstances.

Dharmacari Nagaraja,
member of the Western Buddhist Order

Being old

I don't mind being old, I don't like being perceived as old.

Kenny Rogers, singer and songwriter

The afterlife

A wonderful answer was given to me by my spiritual mentor, Mother Theckla, when I asked her about the afterlife. I remember asking her what she thought about the afterlife and she said: none of my business and none of yours. That's about the best answer.

John Tavener, composer

Stay awake

Sleepin' is the thing which is nearest to dying you'll ever do, so don't do too much of it.

Bill Cullen

Hold to forgiveness; command what is right.

Qur'an 7.199

First Sunday of Advent

As Christians we believe that the Son of God once came to us, we look for him to come again. Make us ever watchful, Lord, that when he comes he will find us ready to follow him, active in his service and joyful in his praise.

Don Maclean

Many answers

My attitude is that there are many answers. We don't get to really know. However we seek more understanding throughout all our lives, even if we know we'll never get it. I don't think our lives are a matter of finding it, knowing it and then living as if we're encased in our knowledge.

Art Garfunkel, singer and songwriter

Master of the day of judgement

All praise is due to God,
The cherisher and sustainer of all the worlds,
Master of the day of judgement.
My Lord, we only worship you, and only turn to you for help.
Please help us stay on the straight path,
On the path of those who have done good,
Not on the path of those who have gone astray.

Khalid Anees
Islamic Society of Great Britain

Unto Allah belongeth the dominion of the heavens and the earth. He giveth life and He taketh it. Except for Him ye hath no protector nor helper.

Qur'an 9.116

About the film *Faithless*

People do miss a dialogue not only with other people, not only with the people closest, but with themselves. And they can look at this movie and see Ingmar Bergmann having a dialogue not only with himself but with all the other characters in the movie. I know that people in the beginning of the film will say, what is this? But when the film is over they are absolutely shattered, they are silent, they are drained. And so many say I am going to be more careful now about the choices in life.

This is not a moralistic movie. This is a film that I hope will shatter you and hope you will decide to do it better. The message is what you find in it. I feel that we lack values today.

People don't go to church; people think, OK, if I do this, life is so short it doesn't matter: why I came to earth doesn't matter because I came for no reason. And this film is maybe showing people that it has a reason. Søren Kierkegaard, the Danish philosopher, said that we come to the world with sealed orders.

Liv Ullman, film director

Great stories

A great production of Shakespeare is something you never, never forget. It sears itself onto your retina. I think children ought to be taken to Shakespeare, not as an exercise in smacking them across the wrist and saying, 'You've got to be educated, my boy', but because you're never going to hear better stories and better human beings tramping about on stage.

Janet Suzman, actor

Don't stop

Don't stop doing things because you're growing old, because you'll only grow old if you stop doing things.

Thora Hird, actor

The Assumption of the Blessed Virgin Mary

Lord, you raised the mother of your son to the glory of heaven. May we be ever mindful of heaven; a share in your glory is our final goal too.

Don Maclean

The Lord said, 'A person always conscious of me, knowing me to be the ultimate aim of all endeavours, the Supreme Lord of the entire creation, and the benefactor and well-wisher of all living beings, attains perfect peace and freedom from all misery.'

Bhagavadgita

Epiphany

On this feast of the Epiphany, when Jesus Christ was revealed to the whole world, we think of the distance travelled and the hardships overcome by the wise men to reach Bethlehem. We pray, Lord, that we will have similar courage and perseverance to overcome any obstacle that prevents us from coming nearer to you.

Don Maclean

Part 2

Living with Others

In the same boat

My grandmother used to say, 'You know, son, in them days we had nothin' and the neighbours, they had nothin' either, but none of us knew we had nothin' because we were all in the same boat.'

Bill Cullen

A natural part of marriage

The atmosphere at home has to be healthy and a positive one. There's no point staying with someone who is making you low, there's an atmosphere at home. The children are going to pick up on this and there's a lot of evidence that it does produce disturbed children. Let's take one common issue in marriage. What is the favourite thing that married people do together? They have arguments.

Conflict is a very natural, important part of marriage. The key issue is how you resolve conflict and there's some very interesting research, where they videotaped a couple having an argument in a laboratory and they found that they could predict who would stay married and who would get divorced seven years later by just watching three minutes of a couple arguing. The point was the way you argued determined whether the relationship survived.

And particularly an argument that escalates. Let's say you were arguing about who does the dishes after the meal and if it immediately escalates that you bring up all the other things with the partner, that escalation seems to predict future divorce. So it seems to be about having an argument about the one thing without throwing everything else in.

Raj Persaud, psychologist

Goodness to others

I won't tolerate people around me or around my children who carry negative attitudes.

I say to my children, you define yourself by your goodness to others, your intelligence, by the way you treat your family, by the way you contribute to society. That is the way you define your manhood, not by having to swagger, not by trying to be bad in order to get your peers to admire you.

Kwame, actor and director

Living for others

As thou, Lord, hast lived for others,
    so may we for others live;
freely have thy gifts been granted,
    freely may thy servants give;
thine the gold and thine the silver,
    thine the wealth of land and sea,
we but stewards of thy bounty,
    held in solemn trust for thee.

S. T. C. Lowry (1855–1932)

None of you have faith unless he loves for his brother what he loves for himself.

Muhammad

God is about love

I'm afraid the way that the churches are going on now – quarrelling inwardly – they make the world think that God is about religion. Instead, God is about love, the world and our neighbours.

David Jenkins, former Bishop of Durham

The heart

The heart that is free of love sickness isn't a heart at all. The body deprived of the pangs of love is nothing but clay and water.

Jami (b. 1414 CE)

A hands-on mother

I have three wonderful girls and I just think if you're a hands-on mother and you watch your children and know what they're doing at all times, you can bring up perfectly fine children there [in Hollywood]. My girls are terrific. I took them to school every day, made them dinner, knew who their friends were. But there are a lot of absentee parents, which is why I wrote a book called *Hollywood Kids*. You see all these movie stars with their kids, and the kids grow up into little monsters or big monsters. There are 22-year-old monsters, you know, going into restaurants and saying, 'My father is so and so, get me a table. Don't you know who I am?'

Jackie Collins, writer

Mothering Sunday

On Mothering Sunday, we remember Mary the mother of Jesus, who stood at the base of the cross on which her beloved son died. May her love be an inspiration and comfort to the mothers of all those who have lost beloved children.

Don Maclean

[Jesus said,] 'Who are my mother and my brothers?' And looking at those who sat around him, he said, 'Here are my mother and my brothers! Whoever does the will of God is my brother and sister and mother.'

Mark 3.33–5

Kids

There's always this umbilical chord between your kids and your wallet.

Jasper Carrott, comedian

For those in poverty

We pray for families whose relationships are under tension and strain because of poverty. For those who struggle to feed and clothe their children, for young people who feel despair as they look for work and for all the victims of poverty who lose heart and hope. We ask that those with the power to bring about change will strive to do so and, if there has been apathy or prejudice in our own hearts, we ask for your forgiveness and for a new resolve to reach out to those who feel isolated and neglected in their need.

Don Maclean

It is the duty of every human being to seek the good of others with his body, mind, words and life.

Bhagavat Purana

Families that share rituals

Religion remains one of the few areas in life that produces rituals. Families that share rituals tend to stay together. So there is something very powerful about events that a family shares. The nice thing about belonging to a religion is that usually at least once a week there's a ritual that the family share.

Raj Persaud, psychologist

A prayer for carers

We pray for carers, particularly for those hard-pressed relatives who are caring for a loved one, a husband or wife, an elderly parent, a child. Pour down your Spirit on them, Lord; give them a sense of humour and help them to keep things in proportion, knowing that you are always beside them. Open our eyes, Lord, that we may look for opportunities to relieve the pressure on carers who are known to us.

Don Maclean

Start at your own doorstep

Where I live, we have a neighbour two doors down. She is an old woman who lives alone. Early in the morning I hear her as she brushes the pavement outside her own house. And then, as she moves slowly past my bedroom window, she sweeps the dirt away from outside of my house. During the day she is often at her door, and she says hello as I come and go. She makes a difference to our little corner of the East End of London. Her care makes it a friendlier place. To be a friend to the world you have to start at your own doorstep.

Dharmacari Nagaraja, member of the Western Buddhist Order

Love the lonely

It is most rewarding to love the lonely and the poor, and to take them as friends.

Ali Ibn Ziyad (eighth century CE)

Hypocrisy

Meekness and modesty are branches of faith, and gossip and the embellishing of facts are two branches of hypocrisy.

From the Hadith

Human relationships

Restorative justice says the purpose of the whole exercise is not so much to be punitive, to try to clobber the perpetrator, as much as saying that the offence has created a breach in relationships. We set high store by relationships, by harmony, the African concept of what is called *ubunto*, which basically is saying that no human being can be human in isolation.

Desmond Tutu, former Archbishop of Cape Town

Remember to forgive

In order to forgive you have to remember, and therefore you cannot expect the Jewish people to forgive the atrocities that were committed against them by forgetting. You can only forgive if you remember. If you've forgotten, by definition, there's nothing to forgive. And this is what is very difficult.

Daniel Barenboim, musician and conductor

[Jesus said,] 'You have heard that it was said, "You shall love your neighbour and hate your enemy." But I say to you, Love your enemies and pray for those who persecute you.'

Matthew 5.43–4

Forgive your enemy

If you get an opportunity and power over your enemy then, in thankfulness to God, forgive him.

Ali-Ibne-Abu Talib (seventh century CE)

Abuse nobody

Abuse nobody, and if someone abuses you, and discloses a vice which they know in you, then do not disclose one which you know in them.

From the Hadith

Karma

I think prayer is part of meditation. I think you can meditate and silently pray at the same time. I think your thoughts are very important and I think your karma is very important. If you are mean to people eventually somebody is going to be mean back to you. And if you have good thoughts about people then it is much better for you personally – for your physical well-being, for everything about you. I'm a very peaceful person. I don't like confrontation. I have good thoughts about people.

Jackie Collins, writer

Pushing boundaries

When you go on pilgrimage you're going to push boundaries.

Ruth Scott, Anglican priest

Therefore do thou give admonition, for thou art one to admonish.

Thou art not one to manage (men's) affairs.

Qur'an 88.21–2

Life is sacred

If you really believe that life is sacred and if you really believe family life is to be ultimately protected, producing new life by allowing people who are infertile to have children, and healthy children at that, is perhaps as important a thing as you can imagine. I'm not arguing that Roman Catholics should do IVF but I think the notion that people who are not of the same faith should impose their view on other people is not acceptable really in a modern pluralistic society given that most people in this pluralistic society are highly moral people. Those who are not Roman Catholic will inevitably take a different view of IVF from those who are, and that seems to me to be completely acceptable. And I think it is the message for our society, particularly now with the strains that it's under; it is so important that we have an understanding of each other, which is why we deliberately shot in the last programme in this series a scene in a mosque because I wanted, as a Jew, to be in a mosque to show that actually that tolerance is a very, very important issue. There are a lot of Muslims in Britain who feel very badly threatened, quite unreasonably, and it is something which we need to be much more aware of.

Robert Winston, scientist

Religious or political?

(*Answering critics who say he is too political.*)

Which Bible do you read? When God delivers a bunch of slaves out of bondage is that a religious or a political gesture? When you read Isaiah, he says that God says, I will not accept your worship however elaborate. Why? You have blood on your hands. You are murderers. OK you still want to talk to me? OK, then show that you have repented and you show how you have repented by how you treat the widow, the orphan and the alien. Jesus said you are not going to be judged by whether you went to church or whether you prayed; you are going to be judged by when you encountered somebody who was hungry you fed them, when you encountered someone who was naked you clothed them. And what is shattering is he says, if you do it to one of these, you do it for me.

Desmond Tutu, former Archbishop of Cape Town

One God

Now that we live in a global village, we should become more integrated into other religious cultures and societies because in my belief there is one God and it doesn't matter how he manifests himself and in what form. People's faith and the way that they wish to express that faith should be at all times respected.

Trudie Styler, wife of the singer Sting

Trinity Sunday

On this Trinity Sunday, we think of the mystery of the Trinity and recognize the essential unity in you, Lord, as Father, Son and Spirit. We too long for unity: in our families, our communities and our churches. As Christians, we follow one Lord and hold a common faith, and yet there are divisions. We look forward to the day when all denominations will bury their differences and become one.

Don Maclean

Limits of reason

Our dad used to say, you can't change a bigot by reason, because he wants to hate someone; he wants to hate someone because they're black, or Protestant, or a Catholic, so even when you've proved to him that he's being foolish, he still wants to be that way.

The Proclaimers, Scottish singers and songwriters

Spirit of openness

Lord, we pray for all who try to speak God's word in a secular age. Grant us a spirit of openness and tolerance towards those with whom we differ and give us courage to stand for what is right and true.

Ernie Rea, former Head of Religious Broadcasting

Love is my law and my faith

Before today I used to reject my fellow human beings if they did not
Profess the same religion as I.
Now my heart is open to every image.
It is a meadow for the grazing deer,
A monastery for a monk,
A temple for idols,
A Ka'ba for the pilgrims,
Torah scrolls and a copy of the Qur'an.
I profess the religion of love,
Wherever its caravan may turn to.
Love is my law and my faith.

Ibn al-Arabi (1165–1240 CE), from *The Tarjaman al-Ashwaq*,
read by Faris Badawi from the Muslim College, London

Mixing with others

A Muslim who mixes with people and bears the inconveniences is better than one who does not mix with them and avoids any inconveniences.

From the Hadith

Corpus Christi

On the feast of Corpus Christi, we remember that you, Lord, kept your people alive in the desert by giving them food from heaven. We give thanks for the gift of the Eucharist, by which you continue to provide for your people. May it serve to unite us as one body in Christ.

Don Maclean

Speak up

Have you heard the one about the visiting preacher who was advised by the churchwarden, 'You have to speak up because the agnostics in here are terrible'?

Charles King, major in the Salvation Army

Love and be loved

Every Puerto Rican loves me, and every Puerto Rican meets me and tells me all the jokes I tell about Puerto Ricans. All the ethnic minorities come to my show and they all love my jokes.

[53]

It all depends on how you mean it. If a person senses hostility they'll hate you for it, if they sense love they'll love anything you say. You can kid your own mother and make fun of her all the time, and somebody else may say the same thing and you might be offended, because you might think they might mean it. It depends who says it and with what spirit it is coming.

Jackie Mason, rabbi and comedian

Trumpet history

Hugh Masekla, the trumpeter, got his first trumpet from Bishop Trevor Huddleston who got it from Louis Sedgemoor Armstrong.

Desmond Tutu, former Archbishop of Cape Town

A waste of energy

Anger and bitterness eat away at your energy. It actually takes a lot of energy to hate someone. You're punishing yourself. If you hold a grudge, if you're walking around hating somebody and seeking revenge on someone, it eats you up. Having the revenge might give you a split second of some kind of twisted satisfaction, but it won't last.

The Barefoot Doctor, Stephen Russell

Peter came and said to [Jesus], 'Lord, if another member of the church sins against me, how often should I forgive? As many as seven times?' Jesus said to him, 'Not seven times, but, I tell you, seventy-seven times.'

Matthew 18.21–2

Marriage that liberates

Marriage is very complicated, but one should feel that one's partner liberates you, but they can only feel like doing that if they feel supported and safe and comfortable in a marriage.

Raj Persaud, psychologist

Love that bears and sustains

On Mothering Sunday we give thanks for mothers and family life. We rejoice in the love, which bears us and sustains us. And we pray for all homes where relationships are strained and frustration leads to anger and fear. We give thanks too for the source of spiritual strength that is the Church. We value those who inspire us by their example and we pray for all who are called to hold authority in the Church and to demonstrate God's care and compassion, that they may be governed by faith and humility.

Noel Vincent, Canon of Liverpool Cathedral

Mercies

God created one hundred mercies and put one of them among His creatures by which they love one another and God has the other ninety-nine.

Imam al-Bukhari (ninth century CE)

A good dad

What makes a good dad? I think ones that talk, get involved. Don't do that thing about sitting in front of the television. Do things with the kids, whether it's going out kicking a football or going out somewhere. Talking and sharing is important: sharing music; sitting down at dinner together; watching the football together; going to the school play and talking about it. Talking about their friends, talking about their first girlfriends, talking about sex. Talking about everything. They know things from a very early age.

Wayne Hemingway, designer

Love and compatibility

If you work at your marriage, your love and affection and strength in a marriage can grow, not deteriorate. People are afraid of making that final commitment because they are worried about how to make that decision and I don't think we give enough guidance about how to make that decision. And I think one of the things is incompatibility. What is it that you couldn't live with? What are the top five things that if a person had, you really couldn't bear it, you couldn't live with that. You need to look at what you can't live with before you actually make a commitment because, fundamentally, if that person you think you want to marry has one of those top five things that you can't abide, that will eventually grind away at the marriage.

Raj Persaud, psychologist

Bind us together

God of our Fathers,
God of our ancestors,
we pray that you will bind us together with your love,
and bind the Church throughout the world.

David Nkwe, Bishop of Matlosane, South Africa

Bring joy

Bring joy into the lives of your friends and meet their needs and respond to cruelty with kindness (such conduct will render all beings your friends).

Ibn al-Husayn al-Sulami (tenth century CE)

Each one is unique

Three times recently somebody has said to me, 'Father, please pray for my son, he is on his way to the Balkans.' Suddenly it is not about so many planes, or so many regiments or a huge number of refugees, suddenly it's a son, a brother, with a mother, father, wife, children. Suddenly, it's not nameless, faceless air crews. It's unique, wonderful, loved, longed-for people; brave or afraid, brash or hesitant, thoughtful, or not daring to think. Suddenly it's names; each one unique.

Pat Kelly, Archbishop of Liverpool

If one member suffers, all suffer together with it; if one member is honoured, all rejoice together with it.

1 Corinthians 12.26

Different needs, different expectations

People are different. People come with different needs and different expectations and it catches them at the most unaware time, when they are not thinking that anything is going on. And we just watch and pick up and pray for people really.

Avril Jackson, spiritual leader

And among His Signs is this, that He created for you mates from among yourselves, that ye may dwell in tranquillity with them, and He has put love and mercy between your (hearts): verily, in that are Signs for those who reflect.

Qur'an 30.21

Coming together

Pilgrimage is the coming together, the sharing of experiences, and what I've found with this particular pilgrimage is that we've come from different traditions. It's very good just to journey along with people of different denominational backgrounds and to get their reflections, their thoughts. Certainly the group I was with were like a family. I feel very sad leaving because you get to know people; it's been a coming together in a very real way and it's been very impressive to see how people have cared for each other.

Oliver McTernan, writer

All Saints

Many of us derive great inspiration from the lives of the saints, or from one saint in particular. Let us remember all those people who have brought inspiration into our lives, be they canaonized saints, teachers, clergymen, nuns, doctors or just ordinary people, that by following their example we may inspire others as they have inspired us.

Don Maclean

The blues is life

The blues was started by the slaves, of course. To me the blues is life; as you're living it, the past and the present, and I believe in the future too. Blues has to do with people, places and things.

B. B. King, king of the blues

Feed a friend

When you feed a friend don't count his mouthfuls.

Muhammad to al-Abzari

The basic question

If you read the book of Genesis, when Cain killed Abel, the Lord had a word with him about it and Cain said, 'Am I my brother's keeper?' That question, 'Am I my brother's and sister's keeper?' is the basic question. Faith is what you'll die for and doctrine is what you'll kill for. I'm not in favour of killing for doctrine, but I am in favour of dying for your faith.

Tony Benn, politician

But forgive them, and overlook (their misdeeds): for Allah loveth those who are kind.

Qur'an 5.13

It stops here

People want revenge and that's perfectly natural and normal to want it, but are we just slaves to these primal forces or do we have a choice to be more evolved than that because, if we're all going to succumb to the urge to seek revenge, then we're just going to destroy each other and there'll be nobody left. It seems, at some point, we have to be big enough to rise above it and say, OK, it stops here. Let the Tao, or let God, or whatever you want to call it, mete out the justice. Because it will. That's the truth. Life will mete out its own justice to people.

The Barefoot Doctor, Stephen Russell

All creatures are God's dependants, the most loved by God are those most helpful to them.

Muhammad

We matter before God

Humanity is created by God in his own image so that each person has worth and dignity. Therefore, we need to pray for a recognition that we all belong together and we matter before God. And out of God we find the grace and ability to deal with conflict and manage it.

Njongonkulu Ndungane, Archbishop of Cape Town

Oneself and others

One should meditate intently on the equality of oneself and others, as follows:

We all equally experience suffering and happiness. I should look after them as I do myself. When happiness is liked by me and by others equally, what is special about me that I strive after happiness only for myself. When fear and suffering are disliked by me, and others equally, what is so special about me that I protect the self and not the other. Therefore just as I protect myself to the last against criticism, let me develop in this way an attitude of protectiveness and of generosity towards others as well.

Vajaisara, from the Friends of the Western Buddhist Order

For the recently bereaved

We ask your blessing, Lord, on all those recently bereaved, particularly those who face the prospect of a funeral this week. Fill them with your Spirit, Lord, and may they be comforted in the sure knowledge of the resurrection.

Don Maclean

Leave us not comfortless

Lord Jesus, before your ascension you told your disciples that you wouldn't leave them comfortless. Be a comfort, strength and protection to those who are lonely or feel unsupported or live in a state of anxiety, and may those whose life is full and secure be supportive to those in need.

Roger Royle, presenter of *Sunday Half Hour* on BBC Radio 2

Muru'a (Compassion)
(from Abdullah Ansari of Heart, The Hundred Grounds)

The elements of compassion are three
Living intelligently with one self
Living patiently with others
Living needfully towards God

Living with Others

Living intelligently with one self has three signs
Knowing ones own value
Seeing the measure of one's performance
Striving for betterment of one's self

Living patiently with others has three signs
Being satisfied with them, according to their abilities,
Being lenient toward their excuses
Giving them justice for their demands, to the extent of your
    ability

Living needfully towards God has three signs:
Gratitude is mandatory for all that happens to you
Recognizing apology as mandatory for all that you do
Recognizing the will of God as right.

Is it from recollection of neighbours in the valley of Dhi
    Salami
That you mix tears with blood as they flow from your eyes?

Or perhaps sweet breezes blowing from Kadhima's
    direction?
Or bolts of lightning that flash in the depths of Mount
    Iddam?

What's wrong with your eyes? You say, 'Stop!'
But only increases their painful downpour;

Or your heart? You say, 'Wake up!'
But it wanders even further in distraction!

Without love's passion you would never have wept so over
    the traces of your beloved's camp,
Nor spent sleepless nights recalling the fragrance of a
    willow or the mountains
your darling walked in

Nor would the mere memory of tents and those who dwelt
    there
Have draped you in mourning clothes, weeping and
    wasting away.

How can you deny such a love, when true tears
And real heartbreak testify so strongly against you?

The sorrow has etched two salty troughs down your face
And branded gaunt marks on it as pallid as yellow and
    blood-red roses.

How true! In the night a vision of the one I long for came
    and deprived me of sleep
But love is famous for impeding pleasures with pain!

O you who fault me for this vestal love, accept my excuses –
Yet if you judged me fairly, you would find me blameless.

May you never have to live like this! I can't even keep it
    secret
From my critics, I'm so feverish and love sick!

You have given me good advice, but I can't hear it –
A lover's ears are deaf to love-critics

How can I listen? I don't even trust the counsel of gray
    hairs,
And everyone knows old age is guileless when it comes to
    good counsel.

Imam Busiri, *The Burda: The Poem of the Cloak*,
tr. Hamza Yusuf (Sandala 2002)

The hand of friendship

Our Father, our King, who has created us all in your image, teach us to see your image in others. Give us the courage to reach out the hand of friendship to all those among whom we live: those who are like us and those who are unlike us, but still like you. Teach us to remember that who is strong is not one who defeats his enemies but one who turns an enemy into a friend, and spread over us all your tabernacle of peace.

Jonathan Sacks, the Chief Rabbi

Friendship

On Monday evening I was flicking through a book called *The Great Songs of the 50s*, just the sort of thing I do when I'm having a quiet night in, and I was grabbed by a song entitled 'Friends and Neighbours'. The lyrics go something like this: 'When you've got friends and neighbours, the world is a happier place. Friends and neighbours put a smile on the gloomiest face. Just take your troubles and share 'em with the folk next door. Makes it twice as easy to bear 'em. It is something money won't buy, although you've not a penny and your house may be tumbling down. With friends and neighbours, you're the richest man in town.'

And I'd even go further than that. Friendship makes the world a beautiful place. Friendship, friendliness can change the world.

Dharmacari Nagaraja,
member of the Western Buddhist Order

Authority

I have respect for institutions but only in so much as they can command our respect, because they can't demand it. It's not theirs by right and I think every institution must be careful not to become a caricature of itself. It's rather like Jesus overturning the moneychangers in the temple. He was bad news for institutions everywhere. I don't know why he's held up as this figure of morality in corporate life because he really wasn't. He was somebody who challenged all of these things and I think that is cause for us to do it in our own life. Authority has to be earned: it's not a gift.

Jeanette Winterson, writer

Common ownership

Permit your friends to claim your belongings as if they belonged to them.

Abu Bakr Muhammad Ibn Zakariya al-Razi (864–930 CE)

Third Sunday of Advent (Rejoice Sunday)

Fill our hearts with joy, Lord, as we prepare to celebrate the birth of the Christ Child. We pray for our family and friends, we thank you for all who care for us and who give us their love. Lord, grant lasting joy to those who give friendship and help in your name.

Don Maclean

Part 3

A Suffering World

The price of hate

Now in the twenty-first century we've just got to learn to live together, because the price of hate gets higher with each decade.

Jonathan Sacks, the Chief Rabbi

Images that convey faith

(*From a discussion about the future of Christianity in the UK.*)

It seems to me one of the reasons why the churches are shrinking is that there's been a failure of the Christian imagination. We can no longer find the images that can really convey faith. And faith is always conveyed through images; it captures the imagination and then from the imagination spills over into the will, and into our actions and so on. Now the writers, the pop groups, the dramatists, the artists are dealing with images that it seems to me we should investigate to find out whether or not there are ways here to get into our theology. That is the area in which much more theological thinking has got to be done. I think we are taking for granted that people will still accept our imagery. We are now three generations away from the people who first stayed away from church and so that imagery has got thinner and thinner. And sometimes it cannot communicate at all.

Remember the Dunblane massacre where all those children were shot. At one of the services, the preacher asked, where was God when all these children were being killed? And his answer was that God was there, suffering with them. Now some people will know that the preacher was talking about the doctrine of the cross and Christ's self-sacrifice, but to people three generations away that sounds nonsense. They don't want a God, who apparently has power and can do all things, just to sit around and let children be butchered. They want it to be stopped.

Colin Morris, preacher and broadcaster

Prayer for young people

Lord Jesus, we pray especially for young people and for all who work with and for them. Lord, during your time on earth your strongest words of condemnation were directed at those who harmed young children. We share your feelings and would seek to encourage and support all who work for the best interests of our young people. Bless them, we pray.

Charles King, major in the Salvation Army

Ground Zero, Easter 2002

I've been to Ground Zero – I'm glad I went.

The area where the Twin Towers once stood is now a void. The two great piles of rubble which we saw so often on our TV screens have been cleared and painstakingly sifted through. Further digging has created a large crater, known as 'The Pit' to those working in it.

To one side are gathered several lumps of unearthed metal, grotesquely twisted, only the wheels giving any indication that they were once cars parked in the underground car park.

All the pieces of steel, which liberally litter the site and everything around it, are blanched a dirty white, presumably from the intense heat. I'm informed that the core temperature was still 2,400 degrees a month after the atrocity. Bodies are cremated at 1,500 degrees, so what hope is there of finding anything of those who died? But I hope they do and, as I watch, a mechanical shovel, like a JCB only much bigger, drops two shovels full of earth, taken from the pit, onto the ground – 'Holy Ground' as Major Mollie calls it. With great skill the operator combs through the earth with the teeth of the shovel, spreading and gently flattening it before withdrawing. Immediately, five New York fire-fighters in helmets, masks and gloves and armed with long rakes move onto the earth and begin raking through it. Frequently they stop, bend and pick up something to examine it more closely. They're looking for body parts, by which they mean bones, or a personal effect, anything which might have survived: a ring, a wallet, a policeman's shield. Ten of those who perished have been identified in such a way during the past few days. There's a priest or a minister of religion on hand at all times in case body parts are uncovered.

God is in evidence here. Overlooking the Holy Ground stands a cross, made from two girders found in their cruciform shape among the rubble. Beneath the cross a small sign says, 'Holy mass here every Sunday 10.30.' To one side someone has recently placed an Irish flag, underneath it the handwritten inscription: 'Lt. Bobby Wallace, I love you Mommy' and a date, 17 March 2002.

I nip into a wooden hut, 'The Hard Hat Café', where Salvation Army volunteers provide coffee and soup for those working their 12-hour shift in The Pit. Young men sit staring into their coffee or straight ahead. The knees of their trousers are worn through, the toes of their boots are worn away too, exposing the steel beneath. On the walls of the cabin are several photos of smiling fire-fighters, written beneath each the word 'found' and a date.

I'm struck by the lengths to which those searching and those supporting them will go, and by their obvious regard for human life, compared with the perpetrators of this vile act who had no regard for life not even their own.

The tallest building in the vicinity, still standing though sorely damaged, is swathed in black netting from roof to ground level. On the side facing The Pit, it boasts an enormous Stars and Stripes flag.

Of all the people I met, I was most moved by Bill Butler, a retired fire captain. He'd been there since September 13th without a break. He's looking for his fire-fighter son, Tom, himself the father of three small boys all under six. He refuses to give up hope. 'I just want to take him home,' Bill said to me. I pray that one day soon he will.

I've been to Ground Zero – I'm glad I went.

Don Maclean

First Sunday after Easter

On Low Sunday we think of Doubting Thomas and Christ's return to convince him. May we be aware that in every believer there is doubt as well as faith. We ask that we shall not feel guilty when we doubt, but that our seeking and questioning will serve to strengthen and deepen our faith in you.

Don Maclean

Human connection

What happens in Palestine affects me in Cape Town. When the Middle East sneezes, we all cough.

Njongonkulu Ndungane, Archbishop of Cape Town

Spirit of peace

We ask your spirit of peace on all areas of the world where there is conflict; may your spirit of reconciliation prevail and the people of violence be shown the folly of their ways.

Don Maclean

Thus says the Lord . . .

They have treated the wound of my people carelessly,
    saying, 'Peace, peace',
    when there is no peace.

Jeremiah 8.11

Forgiveness?

I feel angry that people on our planet could do that to innocent people; it wasn't a military installation; it wasn't that those
people had done something to the people of Afghanistan personally. I know that governments conflict between countries,
but they had nothing to do with it. Innocent people – mothers,
fathers, brothers, daughters – going to work that day, and 78
different nationalities.

I don't know if I'll ever forgive. It's hard to say. My son left
three kids under six years old; they were five, three and we just
christened little Patrick on Sunday. So for a devil's act these
people left a family with three young children. A friend of mine
in Brooklyn – his sister left a building across the street to go to
the World Trade Centre for a meeting and she went up to the
95th floor and the planes hit the building. She was killed: and
she had two young children at home. How long are we going
to continue forgiving, forgiving? It's time to get tough. I'm not
going to forgive for a long time. I don't know if I ever will. I
look at those three little babies and I know that their father
isn't walking in the door. Forgiveness – I don't know, its hard.
It's only six months, it's very difficult.

Bill Butler, a retired New York fire-fighter, lost his son, a fire-fighter, on
11 September 2001.
He came to search for his son at the World Trade Centre one week after the
tragedy. He was still searching six months on.

[Job said,] 'I loathe my life;
    I will give free utterance to my complaint;
    I will speak in the bitterness of my soul.'

Job 10.1

A very sacred place

(*Major Molly Shotzburger talking to Don Maclean, six months after 9/11.*)

I cry a lot. I talk to other people who have been with me from day one. I think what is happening now is that we're just starting to feel the full brunt of it all. We've been so busy and so involved. This is the finality. This is it. You stand with family members and their hearts are just broken; you just can't imagine what they're feeling. I know how I am feeling. You just can't be here and not be touched by it.

Ground Zero is a very, very sacred place. People have been buried here who will never be found. I wear this flag pin and I never want to forget; I want to cherish every day that I have and to give thanks for the blessings that I have. It's just something that will be with me all my life.

Molly Shotzburger, bereavement counsellor,
major in the Salvation Army, New York

A dying mum

Some of the areas in Africa are so bad, there's no running water, no electricity. Just about three months ago we were called to this family. It was dark already and we had to walk a long way, there was no road. And when we got to this little derelict house, only a quarter of it was still standing. I opened the door, it was pitch dark inside and I lit a candle. As we looked on the bed, there was the skeletal woman lying on the bed and rats ran up the side of the wall. As we looked down to see if she was still alive my eye caught a movement down below and

[75]

there were three little children sitting half naked, clutching her bony arm. As our eyes adjusted to the darkness we looked at her feet and rats had been eating her feet. So these children had been sitting in this dark room, cold and frightened with their dying mum; she died later that night. We've taken care of the children.

Heather Reynolds from South Africa,
working for victims of violence and those in poverty

Hold us

God of death who draws all things to an end,
Be with those who grieve in the depths of distress.
Come as the one who understands in the emptiness of
    despair.
Come as the one who revives hope in the loneliness of long
    hours.
Come as the one who brings comfort in the blankness of
    pain.
Come as the one who remembers and through the
    memories sooths the aching heart.
Holy God, our Alpha and Omega, in our living and our
    dying, hold us.

Ruth Scott, Anglican priest

[Jesus said,] 'Blessed are those who mourn, for they will be comforted.'

Matthew 5.4

All war is failure

We look at the children of our own land, innocent, free, hopeful, and we know that they are surrounded by images of pain, war and tears. All war is failure. May we soon say of this war: enough is enough. Any more would be a sin. May we have the humility of God. May we bring our children home to safety. May we find peace. Amen.

Brian Fox, rabbi, Menorah Synagogue, Manchester

Prayer for peace

Give peace to the world, O Lord, we pray; give peace to the victims of war, the refugees, the widowed and the orphans. Give peace to family and friends; to those who've quarrelled and need to be reconciled. Give peace in our own divided hearts. Give peace to us all we pray, in the name of Jesus, the Prince of Peace.

Mark Santer, former Bishop of Birmingham

The end of violence begins with us

(*Commenting on the violence in the USA.*)

We have not done enough to keep people from being mean to people. If people are treated meanly then hostility builds up and explodes somewhere along the line. I bet when they get the people who set off this bomb, I bet they're going to find someone who's been squashed and hurt and humiliated over the years. The truth is even our humour has become meaner and meaner, and this meanness that we are all a part of has to end. So the end of violence begins with us, with us becoming a kinder and gentler people by the grace of God.

Tony Campolo, Baptist minister and
spiritual adviser to former President Bill Clinton

Say no to revenge

I don't think revenge helps anybody; it doesn't justify anything; it doesn't rectify anything; it doesn't undo the wrong that was done. The only way that I think you can actually heal yourself – the situation – however awful it is, is to stop seeking revenge because you have to get to a point, and it's not an easy thing to do, where you don't take personally what was done to you. If somebody else is doing something awful that's their business: it's the best they can be doing at their stage of evolution.

The Barefoot Doctor, Stephen Russell

If you don't forgive

If you don't forgive, then you are condemned to see yourself as a victim instead of seeing yourself as overcoming difficult situations.

Paulo Coelho, author

Give compassion to all in need

Lord, bless all who work to make our nation one in which your name is known and honoured. Confirm those who believe in their faith. Give compassion to all in need.

Ernie Rea, former Head of Religious Broadcasting, BBC

God's mercy

There's a wideness in God's mercy
    like the wideness of the sea;
there's a kindness in his justice
    which is more than liberty.

F. W. Faber (1814–63)

Give people strength

Lord, we pray for all those suffering from depression or anxiety. We pray, Lord, that you will help us to help each other. Give people the strength to overcome the fear of rejection or embarrassment and to realize that help is available if they ask for it. We pray for all support agencies and counsellors working to help people overcome their troubles. Grant them your gifts of patience, wisdom and compassion, Lord, and help us all to trust in you more, to lay our burdens in front of you, secure in the knowledge that no problem is too great or small for you.

Don Maclean

Killed unjustly

(From a multi-faith discussion: 'Was Jesus crucified?')

There's the Qur'anic view that he died and went to heaven. But the question is whether he actually died on the cross. Muslims believe that he did go to heaven and he died. The important thing is that he was killed unjustly.

Halle Afsar, Professor of Politics and Women's Studies, York University

The death of Jesus

(From a multi-faith discussion: 'Who was responsible for the death of Jesus?')

Well, I think it was a combination of political circumstances at that time. The land of Israel was occupied by the Romans; the Romans were very jumpy about possibilities of rebellion; so I think there was a combination between nervous Jewish leaders who felt that Jesus might be causing some trouble and then a savage Roman occupation which acted very decisively once they had identified that Jesus might be a troublemaker.

Why not crucify him? They were crucifying large numbers of people and better get rid of trouble rather than hang about to see what happens to it. But the Jews themselves did not have the authority to sentence anyone to death. Even if the Jews had that authority, by the way, nobody would have sentenced somebody to death for claiming to be the Son of God. I mean we all are. And certainly nobody would have sentenced anyone to death for claiming to be the Messiah. There's been stacks of those before and since.

Clive Lawton, Orthodox Jew and writer

Palm Sunday

On Palm Sunday we think of the fickleness of the people of Jerusalem, who welcomed Jesus with shouts of 'Hosannah' and a few days later were shouting, 'Crucify him.' We pray for consistency in our own faith, that we may not lose heart nor weaken under pressure; that we will never deny you, even under persecution. Strengthen our faith that it will always be there as you are always there for us, Lord.

Don Maclean

Children of Iraq

I want to say a prayer for the children of Iraq and for our community. Pray for the children who now tremble in dark corners with bombs over their heads, our bombs, Iraqi bombs. Our leaders say, 'Children don't be afraid, this is for your own good.' We adults look at each other and we know that we do not know. We can only hope that it is for their good and not for our ego.

Brian Fox, rabbi, Menorah Synagogue, Manchester

Forgive our foolish ways

Dear Lord and Father of mankind,
    forgive our foolish ways!
re-clothe us in our rightful mind,
in purer lives thy service find,
    in deeper reverence praise.

John Greenleaf Whittier (1807–92), poet

Give me another chance

I used to pray to God when I was in terrible shell-fire. I thought my life was going to be taken away from me; I'd become the old Judas, I'd beg and pray like mad. Say please God, give me another chance, let me live, don't let me die this day. I'm the kind of person who could be looked upon as double-faced: one minute saying I don't know, I don't believe God and the next minute calling out for his help.

Don McCullin, war photographer

Church and politics

(*Should senior church ministers get involved in politics?*)

If you're a servant of the Prince of Peace, Jesus Christ, you have no choice.

Denis Sengulane, Bishop of Lebombo, Mozambique

International responsibility

Do you deal with terrorism as a phenomenon or do you look at terrorism as a symptom of deeper problems?

You certainly can't justify acts of suicide bombing. Amnesty International condemns suicide bombings as violations of Israeli human rights. On the other hand, people have a right to resist oppression and a right to resist occupation and colonialism: that's also international law. So the fact that the Palestinians have had to resort to terrorism in order to fight this occupation in my opinion means they have been let down by the international community that has not given alternatives and left them with the only alternative they have, which is terrorism.

Jeff Halper, Ben Gurion University, Jerusalem,
Co-ordinator of the Israeli Committee Against House Demolition

[Jesus said,] 'Blessed are those who hunger and thirst for righteousness, for they will be filled.'

Matthew 5.6

Bless your world

God, bless your world, guide its leaders, guide your children, and give it peace for Jesus Christ's sake.

Denis Sengulane, Bishop of Lebombo, Mozambique

Teach us wisdom

We pray for the violent situations in the world. Be with those whose lives and families have been torn apart by man's inhumanity to man. Teach us wisdom in the way we should pray for the world and for each other. Teach us wisdom in the way we should conduct our lives.

Don Maclean

Our refuge and strength

God our refuge and strength, you have bound us together in a common life, help us in the midst of our conflicts in the world to comfort one another without hatred or bitterness.

Njongonkulu Ndungane, Archbishop of Cape Town

May justice prevail

The Greek Cypriots, from the dawn of Christianity, have been enlightening their lives by the richness of the Gospel. As they carry their cross of suffering they derive strength from the resurrection of our Lord and from the belief that justice at the end will prevail in the world. I wish peace, happiness, fraternity and prosperity for the benefit of the world as a whole. I hope that the Christian principle of love your neighbour as yourself will become the guiding principle of mankind in the new millennium.

President Glafcos Clerides of Cyprus

Requirements for peace

So long as man is captive to his lusts and egotism, follows the way of oppression and tyranny, ignores the commands of heaven, neglects the hungry and sick, does not spread knowledge and justice, and does not deal with people with love and compassion, the long-sought for peace on this planet will never be accomplished.

Sheikh Ahmad Kuftaro, current Grand Mufti of Syria, over 100 years of age

We need forgiveness

Abraham Lincoln said that he never forgave and he never forgot.
This is his way of saying it's all on the permanent track record.
We don't erase what happens, we incorporate what happens.
But forgiveness is what we need to do to our own hurts; to the
things that we do blindly that hurt other people. How can we
live with mistakes made without forgiveness? And if we need
to do it for ourselves – we need to do it to others.

Art Garfunkel, singer and songwriter

What would Jesus do?

My own sense is to try to figure out what Jesus would do. And
how Jesus would handle this. I'm so sorry that Mother Teresa
died because I was in contact with her and we were putting
together a little group of people who, whenever an explosion
took place [in Kosovo], we were committed to go and stand
between the warring sides and say if you're going to kill each
other, you'll have to kill us first.

Tony Campolo, Baptist minister and
spiritual adviser to former President Bill Clinton

Spirit of peace

We ask your spirit of peace on all areas of the world where
there is conflict. But at this time of resurrection, new birth and
hope, may your spirit of reconciliation prevail and the people
of violence be shown the folly of their ways.

Don Maclean

Fear

The biggest casualty of fear is love.

Rhonda Britton, self-help guru

Reflections on death

This coming weekend is an important anniversary in the Buddhist calendar: the Festival of Parinirvanna. It marks the passing away of the Buddha. Primarily it is an opportunity to reflect on impermanence, that all things are impermanent, including you and me. Understanding this is the core of Buddhist practice.

And it is a practice. Death and impermanence are not subjects I would readily turn my mind to if given a choice. But really I don't have choice. For instance, yesterday there was news of a major earthquake, in El Salvador, the second in as many months. On the television I saw images of the aftermath of the earthquakes, the shocked survivors, the bodies of the dead. The pictures of these people passed before my eyes in just a moment. And then they were gone. They passed so quickly. So I did not have time to dwell on what I had just seen and felt it is important to make that time.

Dharmacari Nagaraja, member of the Western Buddhist Order

No easy answers

Whenever a young person dies questions arise. Death raises enormous questions. With our limited human minds, we simply don't know the answers to these questions, and easy answers are normally the wrong ones. In my opinion I have to trust that God knows what he is doing. If I *understood* all that he's doing, I would have to be God myself, so I just trust that there is a point to it all, though we are not able to see it.

Basil Hume, former Cardinal Archbishop of Westminster

A prayer for strength

Lord Jesus, before your ascension you assured your disciples that you wouldn't leave them comfortless. Give comfort, strength and protection to those who are lonely, feel unsupported or who live in a state of anxiety. And may those whose life is full and secure be supportive to those in need.

Roger Royle, presenter of *Sunday Half Hour* on BBC Radio 2

Jesus, my all

Jesus, my all in all thou art:
    my rest in toil, my ease in pain,
the medicine of my broken heart,
    in war my peace, in loss my gain.

Charles Wesley (1707–88)

Real wealth

For many in this world, living in poverty today is a dream in itself. Money is only a means to an end. We cause ourselves and others harm when we see the acquiring of it as an end in itself. The actual problem we each face with regards to money, and what we have to take individual responsibility for, is what we are prepared to do to get it. And then when we have got it, what we then choose to do with it. But real wealth, which is inexhaustible and nothing to do with the bank balance, is a richness of heart and generosity of spirit

Dharmacari Nagaraja, member of the Western Buddhist Order

The cult of bigness

(*From a discussion about the future of Christianity.*)

I still am very suspicious of the cult of bigness. There was a point when the church went astray, when it left its upper rooms and it started building temples to match the Romans. We then got into the whole political thing, and we politicized the Roman Empire. Ever since, our concern has been with success, with getting big numbers, with buildings.

One of the greatest problems the modern church faces is that it has got a whole welter of real estate round its neck that's anchoring it, that is taking up most of its resources. If churches didn't have to pay 90 per cent of their income to keep up buildings, many of which are in the wrong place because populations have moved, the whole scene would be changed. And I think you will be going back nearer to the earlier days of Christianity.

Colin Morris, preacher and broadcaster

Be not hasty

Once, while wandering in a state of anguish, Shebli chanced upon two children tumbling in the dust, brawling over a walnut. He felt called upon to step in and settle the dispute. He broke the nut open, with the intention of dividing it between the two, but he found the shell empty. He broke into inconsolable weeping and cried, 'Oh frenzied soul. If indeed you were blessed with some inner vision you may have the right to apportion shares, be not hasty to presume to be the distributor of shares.'

Islamic traditional

Each generation has its own uncertainties

We live in uncertain times; I read this in a newspaper last week. It said this was a time of economic uncertainty, a time of job instability. It went on to say this is a era of 'collective apprehension'. I must say, I don't feel that. 'Uncertainty' is particular to my generation, to living in the nineties. I was talking to my mother the other night, and she was rejoicing in our national health service, and the progress that has been made in medicine since her day. She told me that during her childhood in Glasgow, it was quite common for children to develop rickets through malnutrition. Babies died of scarlet fever. They even died of measles.

We didn't get around to talking about living through the traumas of the Second World War. What must that have been like? I can't really imagine it. It seems to me that each generation has its own uncertainties to deal with.

Dharmacari Nagaraja, member of the Western Buddhist Order

Bless the people

Almighty God, Creator and Preserver of all, bless the people of this and every nation. Reconcile those who are divided, relieve the hungry and the oppressed; house the homeless and the refugee. Bring joy to the sorrowing, protect and care for the vulnerable. Govern the hearts and minds of those in authority and bring peace and hope to everyone. May your gift of peace flower as love and justice prevail.

John Sentamu, Bishop of Birmingham

Beyond colour

This HIV is beyond colour; it knows no boundaries, it knows no borders. It can cross anytime and I think we need to look at it as not just as an African problem. It is a global problem.

Princess Zulu, Zambian AIDS orphan
and now international spokesperson on AIDS

For those in need

We pray for families whose relationships are under tension and strain because of poverty; for those who struggle to feed and clothe their children, for young people who feel despair as they look for work, and for all victims of poverty who lose heart and hope. We ask that those with the power to bring about change will strive to do so and, if there has been apathy or prejudice in our own hearts, we ask for your forgiveness and for a new resolve to reach out to those who feel isolated and neglected in their need.

Don Maclean

Sleeping rough

We think particularly at this time of those people whose only shelter is a shop doorway: those who suffer the cold, the indignity and the danger of sleeping rough. Help us in our attitude to these poor people and let us be ever mindful that you, Lord, were brought into the world by a couple who had nowhere other than a stable to sleep that night.

Don Maclean

May we reach out

Dear God, let our hearts be broken by the things that break your heart.
Sensitize us to people with the sensitivity that you yourself possess,
and may that kindness and love begin in the homes where we live.
May we reach out from our homes to the larger community.
Dear God, we lift up our hearts to the families who've lost people because of violence. Comfort them with a comfort this world cannot understand.

We trust ourselves into your hands. Make us into good people.

This we ask in your holy name.

Tony Campolo, Baptist minister and
spiritual adviser to former President Bill Clinton

Let our cry come to you

Gracious God, the comfort of all who sorrow, the strength of all who suffer, let the cry of those in misery and need come to you this day, that they may find your mercy present with them in all their afflictions; and give us, we pray, the strength to serve them for the sake of him who suffered for us.

Dan Matthews, Rector, Trinity Church, Wall Street, New York

Great people with huge stature

I really don't like using the persecution that has happened to us, and the Holocaust, which is the worst example of that, as a means to justify hurting other people. I just don't think all those 6 million people died so that we can have Jewish colonies in Palestine. I think there's got to be another answer and sometimes I think we need two 'Nelson Mandelas'. We need two great people with huge stature, one Israeli and one Palestinian, and they can work it out.

Richard Zimmler, writer

Our only helper

O Lord,
have mercy on us at this difficult time.
Let us remember those who are less fortunate than
ourselves.
Let us remember the men, women and children, from
around the world who have lost their lives in conflict.
Have mercy on them, and give strength to the people they
have left behind.
Let us remember those who have been maimed in conflicts
around the world.
Our Lord, help us to help them.
Our Lord, help us to come together, for the benefit of
humanity.
Help us to be merciful, to be compassionate.
Our Lord, you are the most forgiving:
help us to forgive, even when we have been wronged.
Help us, our Lord, for truly you are our only helper.

Khalid Anees,
Islamic Society of Great Britain

If it's easy, it's not forgiveness

Forgiveness doesn't take away justice . . . Forgiveness is an
attitude and there's a process that has got to take place. If it's
easy, it's not forgiveness. Wherever there's real forgiveness,
there's a little cross somewhere.

Chick Yuill, major in the Salvation Army

Forgiveness is virtue, forgiveness is sacrifice and forgiveness is the sacred Vedas. Forgiveness is purity and penance; it is truth, piety, religion, and the Lord himself. Through forgiveness the universe is sustained, and by practising forgiveness a man can attain to everlasting regions of bliss.

Mahabharata

Pray for peace

We pray, Father, for peace; peace in our homes, peace in our hearts and peace in the world where there is justice and forgiveness and love for all; and we pray this in the name of the great peacemaker, your son. Amen.

Chick Yuill, major in the Salvation Army

Listening to the voice of God

Many times fear uses spirituality against us. Let's say you don't know how to make a decision and you're waiting and waiting. 'I'm being patient, I'm waiting on God's answer', while really you've got the answer but you don't want to make the decision; you don't want to take responsibility. Fear uses our spirituality to keep us stuck. Are you really listening to the voice of God and actually doing his will or are you not taking responsibility? Are we using God to expand ourselves and to give us more sense of who we are, or are we using God to keep us stuck in our unhappiness?

Rhonda Britton, self-help guru

Come, Holy Spirit

Come, Holy Spirit, fill the hearts of your faithful and rekindle in them the fire of your love. Such hearts will be restless, fearless, resolute until bombs are silent, refugees return home and no face is bewildered, terrified or lost in the crowd.

Pat Kelly, Archbishop of Liverpool

Brothers and sisters

Father, we turn our hearts to refugees. Soften our hearts we pray and give us the insight to realize that the world you created for us is big enough for everyone and everyone deserves a land to call home, where they can live in peace and safety. Your word tells us to share our good things with others and to treat all men as brothers, all women as sisters. Give us the grace so to do.

Charles King, major in the Salvation Army

A prayer for comfort

We pray for those who, for whatever reason, are on their own today; those who are bereaved or separated by distance or emotional breakdown. Comfort their pain, Lord, and may they invite you into their suffering and find hope in the new life you promise.

Don Maclean

Forgiveness

(The Vicar at Soham said that he finds it hard to forgive. Do you worry that a man of the church has come out with that statement?)

I think that the statement from the Vicar is a very honest statement. I think it was C. S. Lewis who said that everyone says forgiveness is a lovely idea until they have something to forgive. I think we've got to be careful.

Who can offer forgiveness? Clearly it's got to be the victim or the family, and in this particular situation it's the whole community of Soham who need to offer forgiveness, but you know, God's love is unconditional but his forgiveness is not unconditional, I believe. It requires a response of repentance and an amendment of life. Forgiveness needs to be accepted as well as given before it can be complete.

Forgiveness is very costly. You know very well in the case of our Lord himself. He certainly forgave freely but it was at great cost. And he was the victim that actually offered forgiveness. And that's at the heart of true forgiveness. Not something we can anticipate from a distance. I think the vicar at Soham was speaking honestly because although God requires us to forgive and certainly, as a Christian, I don't limit my forgiveness. But at the same time we are human. And the perfection of forgiveness in Jesus may not always appear in us.

Bishop Roy Williamson

God is Religion-Proof

Fortunately God is religion-proof. And no matter what atrocities are done in the name of God you still can find some sort of genuine relationship with whatever that name means.

Jeanette Winterson, writer

In trouble and in joy

Through all the changing scenes of life,
      in trouble and in joy,
the praises of my God shall still
      my heart and tongue employ.

Nahum Tate (1652–1715) and Nicholas Brady (1659–1726);
Psalm 34

Part 4

Seeds of Hope

Music – is that the way East and West will meet?

I no longer think in terms of those kind of boundaries – those barriers of East and West. I think distinctions of nationality are blurring all the time and that can only be a good thing. Nationality can be abused into the manipulation of people to feel insecure about who they are or to feel insecure about people from other cultures. It's much more exciting that we live in a country where diversity is always celebrated and I think that's the way forward.

Nitin Sawhney, writer and musician

God saw everything that he had made, and indeed, it was very good.

Genesis 1.31a

The message is the same

I want to spread the gospel of Jesus Christ in an urban music format. I realized that there were young people out there who would listen to the message if the style of delivery was correct. Jesus said you're fishers of men, and we're gonna change the bait a little bit. The message is the same, but you change the method of delivery. You don't contaminate the message; you don't pollute the message, but if you bring a modern format you will always have young people.

Isaiah Raymond Dyer of Raymond & Co

Love speaks

Beyond words and their meanings, Love speaks
    using another language, different words.
My rival demands 'Say something of Love!'
    but for a deaf heart what can I do but keep silent?
He whose heart is aware of the Lovers' world
    hears nothing but the whisperings of Love –
a tongue unknown to ordinary men.

Javad Nurbakhsh, In The Tavern of Ruin
(Khaniqahi Nimatullahi Publications 1978)

Love is patient; love is kind; love is not envious or boastful or arrogant or rude. It does not insist on its own way; it is not irritable or resentful; it does not rejoice in wrongdoing, but rejoices in the truth. It bears all things, believes all things, hopes all things, endures all things.

Love never ends.

1 Corinthians 13.4–8a

Second Sunday of Advent

Lord, as we spend this season in anticipation and hope of your arrival, we ask you to give us calm moments in which to contemplate the reality of this time. Give us ears to hear the alleluias of your angels, lead us towards the manger and guide us with your star to a place of joy and repose.

Don Maclean

Our complete dependency

Dear Lord, with the world facing war and uncertainty in so many places, help us always to remember our complete dependence on you. Give us the good intelligence to recognize that we are all parts and parcels and that life is meant to know and love you rather than fight over the more than adequate resources you have already provided us. Based on the understanding that you are the one Lord of all faiths and peoples everywhere, help us to work together to achieve a divine consciousness of your ever-loving presence.

Krishna Dharma, writer and Hindu teacher

All my hope

All my hope on God is founded;
    he doth still my trust renew.
Me through change and chance he guideth,
    only good and only true.
      God unknown,
      he alone
calls my heart to be his own . . .

Robert Bridges (1844–1930), poet,
based on the German of Joachim Neander (1650–80)

Thanksgiving for a new day

Father, we thank you for this new day: a day when we awake with hope and new vision to serve and worship you. We pray that our lives will reflect that you are within our hearts and that your will influences everything we say or do.

Bazil Meade, founder of the London Community Gospel Choir

The first music that we knew

It is said that all of nature emulated its sound from the human voice. The human voice is the first instrument, the first music that we knew. It is a shame that we've tethered it into various languages and we are barely able to speak out our laughter or joy any more. We do a lot of Vedic chanting and it is in Sanskrit, which is the cosmic sound, which was put together by the ancient sages. The mind becomes quiet. It makes peaceful the mind; any negative thoughts simply go – they disappear.

Bri Maya Tiwari, Vedic monk

Guide us to the straight way

All praise and thanks is to God alone,
Lord of all that exists,
The most Gracious and most Merciful,
The owner of the day of recompense.
You alone we worship.
We ask for help:
Guide us to the straight way,

The way of those on whom you have bestowed your grace,
Not of those who have gone astray.
O Lord, help us be your hands as instruments of change
within society.
Let us always be an example of good and justice.
O Lord, we are grateful to you for all that you've blessed us
with;
We are fortunate indeed to be in a beautiful country.
Help us, people of faith, to work together to make our
Britain a better more peaceful and just society in which
to live.

Khalid Anees,
Islamic Society of Great Britain

Allah guideth all who seek His good pleasure to ways of peace
and safety, and leadeth them out of darkness, by His Will, unto
the light – guideth them to a Path that is Straight.

Qur'an 5.16

Relieve third-world debt

We think of all who campaign to relieve third-world debt.
Thank you for all those organizers, and for all those who have
signed petitions; we pray that you will give compassion and
care to our governments and other governments to clear these
debts.

Bob White, minister at Poynton Baptist Church

Human rights for all

You can't claim a right for yourself and deny it to others.

Human rights provide a blueprint for a just peace and a blue-print for eliminating terrorism and eliminating the sources of terrorism, because human rights are universal and give every-one a stake in the world.

Jeff Halper, Ben Gurion University, Jerusalem,
Co-ordinator of the Israeli Committee Against House Demolition

Let your steadfast love, O Lord, be upon us
even as we hope in you.

Psalm 33.22

New beginnings

The new year is a time for resolutions and new beginnings. Help us to accept the power of your forgiveness, Lord, and realize that with your love it really is possible to start anew.

Don Maclean

Easter Day

At Easter let us focus on the joy of the resurrection and the power of what was achieved on the cross. Help us always to be aware in our hearts that Christ the Lord is risen today.

Don Maclean

An instrument of peace

Lord, make me an instrument of your peace.
Where there is hatred, let me sow love.
Where there is injury, pardon.
Where there is discord, vision.
Where there is doubt, faith.
Where there is despair, hope.
Where there is darkness, light.
Where there is sadness, joy.
O divine Master,
grant that I may not so much seek to be consoled as to
    console;
to be understood as to understand;
to be loved as to love;
for it is in giving that we receive,
it is in pardoning that we are pardoned,
and it is in dying that we are born to eternal life.

Attributed to St Francis of Assisi (1181–1226)

Looking for a new life

I am a migrant to this country; I'd like to think of myself as proof of what an enlightened immigration policy can do. I hope I have given back as much as Britain has given me. I have empathy with people who look for a new life and I think we're rich enough in this country to have them.

George Alagiah, journalist

Peace be on you: your Lord hath inscribed for Himself (the rule of) Mercy.

Qur'an 6.54

To be forgiving

It is very, very difficult for me, because I've seen so much cruelty, to be forgiving. When you see people cradling their dead children and burying their dead wives the way I've seen in my life, you ask yourself many questions. Why? Why am I seeing this? Why is this happening? These people are at the beginning of their lives. The amazing thing about it is that, amidst all that, you still see people who believe. There is nothing else to cling to.

Don McCullin, war photographer

Holy ground

(*Reflecting on the work of South Africa's Truth and Reconciliation Committee, its chairman, Archbishop Tutu, recalled*)

We've been very careful not to put ourselves out as providing a blueprint for everyone. Situations are unique. But it is possible for people to learn our successes and failures. For me our greatest failure was to be able to engage white South Africans: they were very badly let down by their leaders. They should have had leaders who said to them, 'You don't know how lucky you are. You should engage in this as enthusiastically as you can because the alternatives are quite ghastly and we are extremely fortunate that these blacks who have been victims over so many centuries should be ready to want to forgive.' Those leaders, by and large, were too clever by half, they were splitting hairs and really undermining the whole spirit of the process. Because the whole spirit of the process was generosity. There was generosity on the part of quite a number of people, not just black people, there were white victims too.

I frequently said when we had listened to the testimony of people who had suffered grievously and it had all worked out to the point when the people were ready to forgive, to embrace the perpetrators, I would say I think we should keep quiet now because we are in the presence of something that is holy. We ought in fact, metaphorically, to take off our shoes because we are standing on holy ground.

Desmond Tutu, former Archbishop of Cape Town

Making a difference

Journalists provide information, which allows other people to make a difference.

George Alagiah, journalist

Religion is of the essence

Where was God? What the question really is is a question about *my* theology, *my* understanding and belief in God. What September 11 did was challenge our theologies – all of us. Not just where was God, or where is my God, or the God I believed in as a child. Is that God involved in this? And then to say: Who is the God that the terrorists believe in and have faith and trust in? This is an enormously religious idea. The same God is understood by different people, in different ways. You say you take two children: you say, 'What is your father like?' One child will say, 'My father is very sweet and loving.' The other child will say, 'My father', the same father, 'is mean and difficult.'

September 11 is one of the most profound, theological, God-centred moments in the earth. Because there were people who believed in their God doing what they thought their God wanted them to do.

Attacking a nation that believes it's centred in God. So what is this? These are two understandings of God. That's the reason the Twin Towers disaster is a theological issue.

There are more people who are thinking about Islam than ever before. Some people didn't know what the word *imam* meant until September 11. Now everyone is asking: What is Islam? Who are these Islamic people? What are they like? And we're saying the same things about ourselves. Where was God? Who is the God of Abraham, Isaac and Jacob? Where are we saying the same thing, and where are we saying different things about the nature of God?

To me it is one of the most important things ever to happen in the history of world religion. Because now we no longer have the privilege to indulge ourselves in the idea that somehow I am right and everyone else is wrong. That's an idea we've all grown up with. Roman Catholics are right, Protestants are wrong. Of course everyone knows that, unless you are a Protestant – and then all Roman Catholics are wrong. Here we are growing up with these ideas, almost in a childlike, primitive way, saying, 'I'm right and you're wrong.' Now for the first time, because of the Twin Towers, we're saying, 'Wait a minute, who are they? What do they believe?'

It's an exciting, new possibility that theology will become a part of the conversation of mainstream Britain and mainstream America.

Some of the best articles on faith and religion in the *New York Times* have appeared since September 11. And they didn't write those articles before September 11. Some of those editorial people would say, 'Oh, religion, that's a soft kinda part of life, we don't need to deal with religion.' Religion is of the essence of the world.

Dan Matthews, Rector, Trinity Church, Wall Street, New York

Right there is Calvary

(*Commenting on Ground Zero six months after 9/11.*)

Some of the fellows went in to the Census building, where all the gold was buried underneath, just to survey the area and see how digging could start. The gentleman who led them in happened to be a Christian and, as the folk were following him, he just absolutely stopped in his tracks. They wondered if he'd seen something, or what had happened; they thought maybe they were in danger, so they automatically stopped behind him. Then he motioned for them to come up where he was standing and he pointed to his fellow-workers and he said, 'Look ahead, there's not one but three crosses, and right there is Calvary.' And they all immediately just dropped to their knees.

Molly Shotzburger, bereavement counsellor,
major in the Salvation Army, New York

Reconciliation and rebuilding

I always believed very strongly indeed that resurrection is not just a remarkable thing that happens to the body of Jesus and we all say, 'Oh wow!' But it is something to do with reconciliation and rebuilding, because, when Jesus is raised from the dead, he doesn't just go straight back to heaven and tuck himself up, so to speak. He goes and rebuilds; he goes and meets the people who ran away from him; he goes and gives a commission, a task. I think that it is absolutely essential to believe in the resurrection. It's a gift, it's a task; it's something that enables us to take the memory of suffering on, without being imprisoned by it.

Rowan Williams, Archbishop of Canterbury

Right of sanctuary

Asylum is a sacred right: the right of sanctuary. I went to university in Durham and at the cathedral there there's a big doorknocker, which people can use when they need sanctuary from the state.

George Alagiah, journalist

Islam

Islam insists that all people enjoy freedom of religion and worship. Islam considers sacred all religious places of worship and asks Muslims to defend the right of liberty of worship for all. Islam seeks the establishment of a universal, liberal society in which all can live enjoying freedom in safety and equality.

Sheikh Ahmad Kuftaro, *The Way of Truth*

Losing life and finding it

You asked me is there something distinctive in the teaching of Jesus and certainly one of the distinctive things is that he was always on the side of poor people – against rich people. And one of the central things in the Gospel, which couldn't possibly have been invented because it goes so much against the strain of every way the ancient world looked at life, was that, in order to find life, you should lose it. And in order to achieve riches you should discard all the things which the world esteems as riches – money and power. If you can really do that, which I, of course, can't, you become a strangely powerful being.

A. N. Wilson, writer

I cannot carry this grudge forward

(*Vera Gissing was one of the children brought out of Czechoslovakia – on one of the trains organized by Sir Nicholas Winton – before the Nazis invaded. She was fostered in the UK and lost all her family in the Holocaust.*)

I cannot contemplate forgiveness, not really, when you have your whole family murdered. I don't hold it against Germans of today, but I do hold it against those who committed these terrible crimes. But this problem of mine was eased when I was expecting my second child. I was having this child at home and I had an Irish midwife, and, as can most Irish people, she wormed my history from me. She had a trainee German nurse and, when it came to the actual birth, she let this German nurse deliver my baby and she said to me: you know the Germans have taken so much away from you, I wanted one of them to hand you this new life – your little daughter. And at that moment I felt so small and I suddenly realized I cannot blame the whole nation. I cannot carry this grudge forward; I must be positive and I must look upon the Germans of today from a different angle.

Vera Gissing

Ascension Day

As we celebrate this great feast, we give thanks that our saviour Jesus Christ has ascended on high; and we pray that we too may not be bowed down to the things of this earth, but that our hearts may be lifted up to where Jesus has gone.

Don Maclean

The right kind of life

Judaism probably makes more demands on practice than faith in some sort of way. If you strive for the right kind of life then you are likely to make the right sort of decisions and behave properly. I think that may be true up to a point. It's also unusual in that it's not confined to Judaism, but there is a notion in Judaism that the righteous of all nations should inherit the world to come. So it argues effectively that Judaism is not the only way to strive and I think that is quite a remarkable thing considering it's such an ancient religion

Robert Winston, scientist

I speak Yiddish, I sing Yiddish

(*On receiving the first remembrance award from the friends of the New England Holocaust Memorial.*)

After I sang several songs in Yiddish for the 17 Holocaust survivors that were there and watched their faces light up like children, the man who was responsible for the Holocaust Memorial took me by the arms and shook me and said, you must keep this language alive. And I looked at him and said that I would do what I could. I will try until I die. And I feel very blessed that this massive project, to learn a language that I never knew, was somehow so easy for me to get a hold of once I just had the courage to begin. I speak Yiddish. I sing Yiddish. I can go to a Yiddish-speaking film or a German film and understand 30 to 50 per cent of it. The Hebrew language is the language the Torah and the Talmud is written in. It's the language of prayer, the language you speak to God in. And Yiddish was a street language, comprised of ancient German, Polish, Russian and other pieces of other languages as this travelling tribe moved around. I prefer not to call it a dying language, but a struggling language. One of the joys is that my son, both my sons, learned all this Yiddish music faster than I did.

Mandy Patinkin, singer

Your good gifts

Help us to look for all your good gifts in our lives: the big ones and the little shafts of light too, and to celebrate them.

Anne Easter, Anglican priest

God winks

Every time a coincidence happens to you or an answered prayer or one of those things which makes you say, Wow! What are the odds of that happening? That is a 'God Wink', a little message of reassurance directed to you, like a signpost on the highway. I believe that we are directed – we are on a global position-ing system at all times and that our lives are really directed by many of these little messages. Just as we need to pay attention to the signposts on the road to make sure we are on the right path, we need to pay attention to the 'God winks' just to make sure that we have a connection.

First of all we all have a destiny, it's like a DNA, it's there, but most people don't reach their destiny because they sit by the side of the road and wait for their destiny to come to them. But if we get on that highway of our life, heading for what we believe to be our destiny, our hands are round the steering wheel most of the way. We just need to pay attention to the signposts – those little 'God winks' of reassurance: 'Hey kid keep going, I'm thinking of you, hang in there.'

Squire Rushnell, author of *When God Winks: How the Power of Coincidence Guides Your Life* (Simon & Schuster 2003)

The King of love

Perverse and foolish oft I strayed,
> but yet in love he sought me,
and on his shoulder gently laid,
> and home rejoicing brought me.

H. W. Baker (1821–77); Psalm 23

On the beach in Cyprus

Ah! This is the life. I'm waist deep in the Mediterranean at Aya Napa. Most people under the age of 25 will know about Aya Napa. Every summer thousands of youngsters flock here to enjoy not only the sea and sand, but also the clubs and discos which provide a nightlife to equal anything Ibiza has to offer.

I'm wading ashore now, as St Barnabas and St Paul probably would have waded ashore in about AD 45. It is recorded in the Acts of the Apostles – I'll just consult my waterproof Bible.

'While they were worshipping the Lord and fasting, the Holy Spirit said, "Set apart for me Barnabas and Saul"' – that's St Paul before he changed his name – '"for the work to which I have called them."' Then a bit further on it says: 'When they arrived at Salamis' – that's further up the coast – 'they proclaimed the word of God in the synagogues of the Jews.'

There's great devotion to St Barnabas here in Cyprus. He was a local lad. Born here. He and Paul went to Paphos, on the west coast of the island, and there they so impressed the Roman Governor, Sergius Paulus, that he converted. He was the first high-ranking Roman to become a Christian. It's said that St Paul changed his name, from Saul, at that point. St

Barnabas became the first bishop of the Cyprus church. He ordained other bishops, including Lazarus – the brother of Martha and Mary – whom Jesus had raised from the dead. He died for the second time in Larnaca. He stayed dead that time. Barnabas too died here. Actually, he was martyred. His killers built a huge fire and threw his body on so that nothing of him would remain, but the flames did not touch his body and the body remained intact. Spooky or what?

The name Barnabas means 'son of encouragement'. It says that in the Bible too. Barnabas encouraged the Cypriot people to embrace the Christian faith which they did then and are still doing today. It's wonderful to see how religion is very much a part of everyday life here. No wonder that Cyprus is known as the island of saints.

Don Maclean, during an Easter broadcast from Cyprus

Too much

I think if I was to draw up a list of the 20 places in the world that I would most want to visit before I die, I've probably seen almost half of them on this pilgrimage. It's almost too much to cope with sometimes. Imagine you're standing on top of Mount Nebo and seeing exactly the site that Moses saw. Standing on the shore of Lake Galilee, probably at the very spot where Jesus forgave Peter, was for me very, very real, because it just looked so natural; there was almost nothing that wouldn't have been there when Jesus and Peter were standing there. And to do it in company with other people who share the same ambition and hopes has been tremendous, all sharing this dream of coming to the Holy Land. It's been a dream of a lifetime but the reality is so much better than the dream.

Charles King, major in the Salvation Army

Morning has broken

Morning has broken, like the first morning;
    blackbird has spoken, like the first bird.
Praise for the singing! Praise for the morning!
    Praise for them, springing fresh from the Word!

Eleanor Farjeon (1881–1965)

An Easter reading

Let us who have beheld the resurrection of Christ, worship our holy Lord Jesus who is alone without sin. We worship that cross, O Christ, and praise and glorify that holy resurrection. For thou art our God and we know none other beside thee and we call upon thy name.

Come all ye faithful, let us worship Christ's holy resurrection, for behold, through the cross, joy has come to the whole world. We praise his resurrection and forever glorify the Lord. He endured the cross for us and by death destroyed death. Jesus, having risen from the grave, as he foretold, has given to us eternal life and great mercy.

Greek Orthodox Easter reading

Looking

I think the mere silencing of the mind when you look long at a picture is a prayerful thing because all great art is spiritual. Look at a great Degas ballet dancer – look at it well and see the beauty of the body and the reverence in which she is painted, everything about the dancer's movement and colour and setting, and you will come close to God.

Wendy Beckett, nun and art critic

The sunrise of faith

My birth certificate reads English, Arabic and Hebrew, and we lived in peace. What went wrong? But again this is the sunrise of faith. This is the cradle of the three monotheistic religions. Let's get together now as we are and try and make it together.

Aktel Biltazi, Jordanian Minister of Tourism

How can you be so joyful?

I've always been this person who never questions God. I think of God as sovereign and bigger than us. How could I ask my Maker where are you? What is this? When I learned that I was HIV-positive, I had a personal relationship with Christ and one thing that came to me was just to thank God in the middle of the situation, and instead of me breaking down, I decided to break through. Many people say, what are you talking about? How can somebody be so joyful? But for me I think it was more of an inner thing, a spiritual reaction. I believe that God has called me at such a time like this to be a voice to millions of people infected with HIV or AIDS.

Princess Zulu, Zambian AIDS orphan and
now international spokesperson on AIDS

The strength of goodness defeated

If there's one thing Good Friday and Easter can teach us is that goodness defeated is stronger than evil triumphant. It was Martin Luther King who said that. So often when you see these barbaric acts that have been happening in recent days you sometimes feel, oh dear, evil seems to be supreme. Goodness seems to be lost. Goodness defeated is stronger than evil triumphant and that's what the resurrection is all about. God doesn't give up on us. Failure is not the last word. So Jesus rose from the dead to reveal that goodness will triumph over evil in the end. And therefore I would long for the peacemakers and all people of goodwill to keep their eyes on the cross and resurrection: therein lies the hope of all the ends of the earth.

Roy Williamson, former Bishop of Southwark

God can use suffering

I don't believe for one minute that God creates suffering as a test of faith but I do believe that his will can use suffering and apparent failure to bring blessing to very many.

Noel Vincent, Canon of Liverpool Cathedral

God knows best

(Reading from the letters of a Sufi master.)

There are many signs by which those who have reached God may be recognized, namely that all things great or small are in their hands and under their control for they are to the universe as the heart is to the body, but God knows best.

Read by Abdullah Trevathan, Headteacher of Islamia School

Out of the ashes

We all know that out of the ashes will come new beginnings, new hope. That's exactly what Easter is all about. Our fundamental belief is that out of death comes life, out of destruction comes hope. We know that. It happens to us in our lives in little ways sometimes. Gosh! I thought this was a tragedy, but it turns out to be the best thing that ever happened to me. I lost my job. I cried and cried over losing my job: lo and behold I've found a better job than I ever thought I would ever have. We know that all the time.

Dan Matthews, Rector, Trinity Church, Wall Street, New York

The Transfiguration

It is the feast of the Transfiguration, when Jesus appeared in heavenly glory before his three closest disciples. Fill our lives, Lord, with some of that light so that we may be dazzled anew by your power and majesty.

Don Maclean

In heaven and on earth

The living Church is not just the people living on the earth; it is also the people who have passed away. All people – the Church on the heaven and the Church on the earth – are together. So when we pray in the church, surrounded by these icons, it means that all people are there gathered round the table of the Eucharist.

Father Vasilika, the Greek Orthodox Church in Cyprus

Cobras and archdeacons

The floods in Mozambique have been a tragedy and a miracle. Let me tell you how God has intervened in the situation to open our eyes. We have one of our archdeacons, the Archdeacon of Limpopo, who fled from his house. The only thing which he was able to grab was his surplice. The water was coming behind him. He climbed on a tree and, as he reached the branches, he looked down and he saw a snake trying to climb the same tree. So he used his surplice to stop the snake. He hit the snake and the snake fled, but he looked up and on the top of the tree was a cobra, a big snake. So there was nothing he could do but to negotiate with a cobra. Two of them shared their shelter provided by God. Of course, it is not normal for a cobra to climb on trees, but I would say archdeacons don't normally climb trees. But the two of them shared this shelter. God provided for them for two and a half days. We have many stories of divine intervention. We must recognize that God is flooding the country with acts of generosity from both inside and outside the country.

Denis Sengulane, Bishop of Lebombo, Mozambique

Keeping Jewish Law alive

(*From an interfaith discussion on Christianity.*)

Jesus was a radical Pharisee, observing the Jewish Law, coming up with interpretations, which are challenging and creative, which was exactly what the Pharisees were doing. The interpretative process is that which keeps Jewish Law alive. The New Testament casts a particularly sharp eye on this one moment and this one person. Read the Talmud and you find a thousand rabbis arguing similarly.

Clive Lawton, teacher and Orthodox Jew

Ways of war

In the battle of Siffeen, Mu'awiya reached the Euphrates before the army of Hazrat Ali and took possession of the bank. When Ali's forces approached they were informed that they would not be permitted a drop of its waters. Ali sent word to Mu'awiya that this was against the 'Canons of Humanity and the orders of Islam'. Mu'awiya replied: 'War is war and one cannot therefore accept such principles, seeing, as it is my aim to kill Ali and to weaken his army, this stoppage of water will accomplish my aims quickly and easily.' Ali sent Hussain to gain the bank which objective his forces swiftly attained. It was Mu'awiya's turn to plead access to the river. Ali told them to take as much as they wished and to return as often as they liked.

From Ali-Ibne-Abu Talib, *Nahjul Balagha* (Peak of Eloquence)

The attainment of peace

But Islam, in controlling the use of force in the direction of creating equilibrium and harmony, limits it and opposes violence as aggression to the rights of both God and His creatures as defined by the divine Law. The goal of Islam is the attainment of peace but this peace can only be experienced through that exertion (*jihad*) and the use of force which begins with the disciplining of ourselves and leads to living in the world in accordance with the dicta of the *shar'ia*. Islam seeks to enable man to live according to his theomorphic nature and not to violate that nature. Islam condones the use of force only to the extent of opposing that centripetal tendency which turns man against what he is in his inner reality. The use of force can only be condoned in the sense of undoing the violation of our own nature and the chaos which has resulted from the loss of equilibrium. But such a use of force is not in reality violence as usually understood. It is the exertion of human will and effort in the direction of conforming to the Will of God and in surrendering the human will to the divine Will. From this surrender (*taslim*) comes peace (*salam*), hence *islam*, and only through this *islam* can the violence inbred within the nature of fallen man be controlled and the beast within subdued so that man lives at peace with himself and the world because he lives at peace with God.

Seyyed Hossein Nasr, 'Islam and the Question of Violence'
in *Al-Serat*, vol. III, no. 2.

Disarmament on biblical principles

(Recently the Bishop received the CMG and also the All Africa Congress of Churches Peace Award for his work as a peace negotiator.)

An award is really an agenda which is set before you to say you can do it. So it was in that context, because we were involved in bringing together the Renamo and Frelimo in Mozambique to talk to one another, and now we have reached peace in Mozambique.

But before we reached peace, we realized that there were so many guns in the hands of people therefore we needed to do something about it. So when the peace award was given, we said let's not hang it on our wall but let's hang it in the hearts of people. And it was in that context we conceived what is called the 'Swords into Ploughshares' project. What is it? It is disarmament based on biblical principles. We encourage people who have guns to bring them and if it is a working gun we exchange that gun for a sewing machine or a plough or a bicycle or building materials. We are saying, go and use your skills and your ability to build peace rather than use an instrument of destruction. And we have collected more than 75,000 different items of war.

Above all we would like it to appeal to armament manufacturers, that you could transform your skills to make guns into skills to make instruments promoting human dignity, of declaring sanctity of life. We are saying stop the war, not tomorrow, not this afternoon but now in Angola. Stop sending guns to Angola. If you don't know what to do with them, give them to us and we'll cut them into small pieces and then send them to a place where they can be melted down and made into instruments of production.

Denis Sengulane, Bishop of Lebombo, Mozambique

Forgiveness in Africa

Forgiveness is part of the culture of Africa.

George Alagiah, journalist

Nurturing friendship

In Buddhism the cultivation of friendship is a central spiritual practice. I know that in my own life so much of what I have achieved has been made possible by the support and encouragement of my friends. And that the darkest times in my life have been when I felt that the world has forgotten me and I am alone, and it is not easy to make friends, or to keep them. It is not something that can be hurried. Friendship needs time and patience and commitment if it is to flourish and grow.

Dharmacari Nagaraja, member of the Western Buddhist Order

God's constant love

Thank you, Father, for your love that stays constant and stays unchanging. We pray for all those today who feel under the weather, where changes have come in their circumstances. We pray that they may know your love which stands like a shelter, stands over them, that doesn't alter even if they do something wrong. Thank you, Father.

Rob White, minister at Poynton Baptist Church

Say: 'If ye do love Allah, follow me: Allah will love you and forgive you your sins: for Allah is Oft-Forgiving, Most Merciful.'

Qur'an 3.31

To see the world as God sees it

Prayer is essentially standing naked before God with our arms open, and allowing our hearts to descend into the heart of God. And if we do this it enables us to see the world as God would see it and therefore gives us that courage to work for the well-being of humanity and for the goodness of God's creation.

Njongonkulu Ndungane, Archbishop of Cape Town

Balance the scales

(*If £1,000,000 were to land on your lap tomorrow, what should you do with it?*)

Think about one thing you could do to make someone else's life better and make one of your dreams come true. I always think that if you give the same amount of money away that you spend on your dream, the scales in life are balanced.

Alvin Hall, financial guru

Thy kingdom come!

Thy kingdom come! On bended knee
    the passing ages pray;
and faithful souls have yearned to see
    on earth that kingdom's day.

F. L. Hosmer (1840–1929)

[Job said,] 'I know that my Redeemer lives,
    and that at the last he will stand upon the earth.'

Job 19.25

Windows into heaven

Icons tell us something about what Christ is, what the Mother of God is. I suppose I see them as windows into heaven, as it were. It is as near as we can get to heaven – that's why we kiss the icons and why we make the sign of the cross. And even if you look at a very primitive Greek icon, like this one of Christ, which was found in Paul McCartney's dustbin by my brother. This was not because Paul McCartney had any aversion to icons, but clearly, I think, when The Beatles visited Athens, they were showered with icons and he probably didn't want all of them.

John Tavener, composer

Reflecting on impermanence

Although Buddhism teaches that we should reflect on impermanence, that all things change, even ourselves, it does not see this as a depressing or undermining practice. But rather the Buddhist attitude is that if we embrace impermanence and live our lives with awareness of things as they really are and not as we want them to be, we will appreciate that our time here is limited. And we should not take things or other people so much for granted. Every moment becomes precious. Every meeting and parting. The times we are in the company of loved ones, our colleagues, are times to be cherished and enjoyed. If we can achieve this, we may truly begin to live.

Dharmacari Nagaraja, member of the Western Buddhist Order

Let peace come

Almighty God, we know that without justice there can be
   no peace.
Let peace come when all peoples are respected, regardless
   of race or religion.
Let peace come when trading weapons of mass destruction
   is a crime.
Let peace come when the earth's resources are used wisely
   for the common good.
Let peace come when money is used to serve and not
   enslave the world.
Let peace come through the transformation of our lives
   that we may do justice, love and kindness and walk
   humbly with our God.

Ruth Scott, Anglican priest

Sunsets become dawns

Clement of Alexandria said, because of the risenness of Jesus, God turns our sunsets into dawns.

Michael Bowering, Archdeacon of Lindisfarne

Lord, we remember

Lord, we remember all those whom we love who've gone to be with you. Lord, we rejoice to know that your love extends far beyond the limits of this life in the mystery that lies beyond our sight. We pray that your love may complete its work in those whose days on earth are done and grant that those who serve you now in this world may at last share with them the glories of your heavenly kingdom.

Ernie Rea, former Head of Religious Broadcasting, BBC

Death overcome

Death's mightiest powers have done their worst,
and Jesus hath his foes dispersed;
let shouts of praise and joy outburst:
Alleluia.

Latin, probably seventeenth century;
trans. Francis Pott (1832–1909)

The highest perfection of human life, achieved either by complete knowledge of matter and spirit, by practice of yoga

and religion, or by perfect discharge of duty, is to remember
the Supreme Lord at the end of life.

Bhagavat Purana

Resurrection

Lord Jesus Christ, you are the Resurrection and the Life.
Live in us, we pray, with your undying life;
that we may live for you and for one another,
now and always. Amen.

Mark Santer, former Bishop of Birmingham

All gains will end in loss, every meeting ends in separation and
all life has its end in death. As there is no fear for a ripe fruit
other than a fall, so there is no fear for any man other than
death. Therefore dedicate your life to achieving immortality
through service to the eternal Supreme Lord.

Ramayana

A traditional blessing

May the road rise to meet you.
May the wind be always at your back.
May the sun shine warm upon your face,
The rains fall soft upon your fields.
And until we meet again, may God hold you in the palm of
his hand.

Traditional Celtic blessing read by Maddy Prior, singer and songwriter